The Green Cowboy

An Energetic Life

S. David Freeman

authorHOUSE®

AuthorHouse™
1663 Liberty Drive
Bloomington, IN 47403
www.authorhouse.com
Phone: 1 (800) 839-8640

Published by AuthorHouse 10/24/2016

ISBN: 978-1-5246-1743-1 (sc)
ISBN: 978-1-5246-1744-8 (hc)
ISBN: 978-1-5246-1742-4 (e)

Library of Congress Control Number: 2016910985

Print information available on the last page.

This book is printed on acid-free paper.

This book is dedicated to my parents,
Lena and Morris Freeman.

Only in America could I, a son of Lithuanian immigrants, become the first "native" Tennessean chairman of the board of directors of the giant Tennessee Valley Authority (TVA), one of President Roosevelt's most successful New Deal agencies.

Both of my parents were Jewish, born in different small villages in Lithuania. Dad came to America in 1906; Mother in 1924. Dad first lived in Worcester, Massachusetts. He learned to repair umbrellas. Upon receiving a letter from a cousin in Chattanooga, Tennessee, saying it rained a lot in that town, he moved there. Mother went to Atlanta, where her two older sisters lived. Through a mutual friend, a modern-day matchmaker, my mom and dad first met in Dalton, Georgia, a small town about halfway between Atlanta and Chattanooga.

My parents lived the American dream. They worked hard, loved their kids, sent them to college, acquired a small home of their own, and were proud of their country and their family. I regret that my father, who was a Socialist-turned-New-Deal-Democrat, did not live long enough to witness his son become the chairman of the TVA board, a truly Socialist agency that he admired. But my mother did, and for that, I am thankful.

There are two important appendices to this book. Appendix A is a short history of my dad's (and my mother's) life that I wrote in the seven days of *shivah* (mourning) after his death. Appendix B is a collection of some of my mother's funny remarks, which I remembered in the days after she passed away.

When I was growing up, my Southern accent had a Yiddish flavor to it, but I felt no discrimination from the Christian white people in Chattanooga, Tennessee, where I grew up; in fact, their expectation of me as a Jew was that I had superior knowledge of the Bible. Instead, they directed all their hate toward black people. The only time I felt different was during Christian Bible class—which was taught right in the public school—because my parents wouldn't let me attend. I went to study hall instead and did my homework, which was fine with me. All school relationships stayed friendly. The public school Bible teacher, Mrs. Flynn, came to my bar mitzvah. It was an all-white, happy-family environment.

I joke that the only discrimination I felt, as a Jewish son of the South, came from my mom, who forbade me from dating non-Jewish girls. This Jewish mom attitude really was unfair to the Jewish girls in Chattanooga. At school dances, I always went stag and cut in on all the cute non-Jewish gals; that was an acceptable custom. The Jewish gals largely stayed home because girls didn't come to school dances without a male date in those days.

We lived in a poor neighborhood where black and white families lived close to each other. Until I went to school at age six in 1932, most of my friends were black kids. We played together all the time. But the segregated schools caused us to part company. It wasn't just the schools that were segregated—every facet of life separated the races. Drinking fountains had signs that said WHITE ONLY. It was the same for restaurants. Black people weren't allowed in public toilets, and state liquor stores even featured plywood separators.

As a Jew, with parents who had been exposed to even worse treatment in the old country, I was sympathetic to the plight of black people. Yet, as a kid, I didn't do anything about it. I was just glad people were not mean to me. My understanding of the plight of black people did grow from passive to active when I was thirty. I actually sat in at the lunch-counter demonstrations in Knoxville, Tennessee, where I was working as an engineer for TVA. The angry white people called me all kinds of bad names, and I must admit after a few days of showing my support, I stopped showing up. But my interest in advancing civil rights continued.

To say my early years were uneventful would be an exaggeration. I was a timid kid with adoring parents who gave me unquestioning love and no rules. Nothing was said, but I understood I had to behave and make good grades, which I did. My mother did not allow me to skate or bike because a cousin in Atlanta had broken her ankle skating. They stopped me from doing things they thought were dangerous yet I had no rules about when I had to come home or what I did in or out of school. My parents gave me all the freedom in the world, but I was too shy and insecure to take advantage of it.

Folks who encountered me later in life may have had a hard time believing I was a good boy who never really gave my parents trouble. But that's how I was as a kid, except when I almost got in trouble one Halloween night. Perhaps out of boredom, I was about to throw a brick at a streetlight, when, out of nowhere, a police car came screeching to a halt in front of me, with the cop yelling, "Get in!" He then started driving—I thought toward the police station. I was not as scared of the cop as I was of having to call my dad from jail.

After driving me several blocks, the cop said, "Son, if I let you out, do you think you can find your way straight home?"

"Yes, sir!" was my joyous answer. And I did run home.

As a kid, I played touch football and softball and hiked in the nearby mountains. I was not sickly, but I had asthma—which I outgrew. I learned to hate coal at an early age, since I had to shovel it into the furnace that heated our house. And I still have a vivid memory of when we lived near railroad tracks and the coal-fueled trains belched black smoke that triggered my asthma. My asthma actually caused my parents to move us to the countryside, as they spent their lives devoted to my brother Harold's and my welfare. There, we had no family car; my dad rode the bus to work, and Mom was isolated. I had fresh air, nearby kids to play with, the experience of going to a country school with an outhouse for a bathroom, and the memory of a wild horseback ride on a friend's nearby farm.

I essentially grew up as an only child, since I had no sisters and Harold, my only brother, was seven years younger than me. The age gap kept us apart. By the time he was more than just a kid brother, I was out of high school and gone. However, I had one incident with him that I'll never forget. When we first moved to the country just outside of Chattanooga, as I pushed the buggy in which the very young Harold was lying, we hit a bump. He somehow slid out of the buggy and fell into the grass. It scared me to death because I feared I had really hurt my baby brother, but he didn't get hurt. Our mother calmed me down. I don't recall that Harold even cried, but I had never been so scared that I had screwed up in all my life.

I played a lot of tennis as a kid, since the nearby public courts were free and I wore tennis shoes anyhow. Another one of my favorite pastimes was walking a mile to Southern League baseball games, as they gave us kids free seats in the third base–line bleachers. They called us the Knothole Gang. If we had a nickel for candy, we felt lucky. The team that played there, the Chattanooga Lookouts, is a farm team of the Washington Senators, who we hated because they would call up the Lookouts' best players in the middle of the season.

In junior high, I made the basketball team but sat on the bench almost the entire time. I was on the track team but only participated on the relay-race team. The big event I recall from junior high is we got out of school one afternoon to see *Gone with the Wind.*

In high school, I did not get good enough grades to make the honor roll. I was too short to make the basketball team. I worked for the school paper but only as advertising manager. I also joined ROTC and made second lieutenant.

With girls, I was shy, not popular. In those days, boys and girls were not "just friends." My friends were all guys. The only girls I knew as a kid were the very few girlfriends I had. And with no family car, I was dependent on male friends to double-date. I do remember going on dates on the streetcars, or trolleys, which have long been abandoned, but my love life as a kid was, by present-day standards, more of a dream than a reality.

My one claim to fame in high school was that I was selected to go to Boys State, where kids from all over Tennessee got organized into a mock state government for a week. I was a member of the state supreme court. We learned a lot about government functions. Maybe it provided a sign for my future career, but that didn't register at all at the time.

My first big trip in life took me to New Orleans as part of a debate team. The debate topic was "Released Time for Religious Education: Is It Constitutional?" The topic interested me since I had encountered the opposite of that proposition when I avoided religious education in school. My work on the debate team was an early sign I had arguing skills, not engineering skills—a sign that was lost on *this* high school student.

My male friends and I celebrated high school graduation by renting a truck and filling the truck bed with hay. Our hayride with our dates lasted until 3:00 a.m. I was such a klutz that I lost my date Gerry Daneman's house key. I had to wake up her father so she could get back into her house—and that ended my last chance for high school romance.

Everyone remembers his or her whereabouts on and reaction to Pearl Harbor Day, December 7, 1941. I was in high school, and I clearly recall that a bunch of us, all guys, were sitting around talking on the porch at the Jewish community center when we heard the news. Our unanimous reaction was regret that we were going to miss fighting in the war. We thought that the "crazy Japs" had picked a fight with the mighty United States and they would get licked in six weeks. Little did we know that most of our Pacific Fleet was at the bottom of Pearl Harbor and we had a long struggle ahead of us in which some of us would get killed.

My high school days were a time when America was at war. Partying was tame by modern-day standards. We collected scrap tin for the war effort, an early exposure to recycling. We took our ROTC training very seriously since we all were anxious to join the war effort. We took learning to march in unison as seriously as any of our courses.

OFF TO THE WAR

World War II was well underway when I graduated from Chattanooga High School in May 1943 at age seventeen. I knew I was going to war, but I did want to get started in college that summer. I chose Georgia Tech, an engineering school, because someone said I should become an engineer since I was good at algebra and engineers were in demand. That was by far the worst career advice anyone ever got.

I did well as a freshman, but I faced an early draft into an army replacement training center and would no doubt have seen duty in the battles that took place in Germany in 1944. My interest in serving my country did not include being in the army infantry. My preference for where to serve was not motivated by fear but rather by the desire to become an officer with the kind of uniform that attracted pretty girls.

I first applied to become a naval aviator in the navy's V-12 program but was rejected because of my overbite; at that time, V-12 program required a perfect bite to handle the face masks pilots used when flying. Then a frat brother at Georgia Tech named Joe Schwartz told me of the Merchant Marine Cadet Corps, which had pretty uniforms. The duty was at sea on merchant ships for a year and was followed by attendance at the Merchant Marine Academy at King's Point, New York. Admission was by state quota. No one from Tennessee knew about it.

Even though I had never even seen the ocean, I applied and was accepted. I made this decision against the advice of my father, who made a special trip to Atlanta to talk me out of it because the merchant marines were losing so many ships to Nazi submarines.

But to my mind, a pretty uniform and a warm bed won out over foxholes.

After brief basic training at Pass Christian, Mississippi, I went aboard a newly built ten-thousand-ton tanker that transported high-octane gasoline for airplanes. We made three round-trips across the North Atlantic delivering aviation fuel to the air force in England and Italy. These trips across the ocean occurred in 1944, when the submarine menace had abated but was still very real. I was lucky that our ship was never hit, but I still remember the sound of the depth charges dropped by navy destroyer escorts protecting our country. I saw oil slicks showing that the navy destroyer escorts protecting our convoy had sunk a nearby Nazi submarine.

My first encounter in the London occured when I left my ship at night and found everything dark. The City was under attack from the German air force and there were no lights on. The first sound I heard in that very dark street was with a man on the corner shouting, "Flashlights, condoms!" the two best sellers in the London blackout. I didn't buy either, having been scared by the movies we had been shown that revealed the horrible results of venereal diseases resulting from sexual activity.

My most vivid memory of my North Atlantic sea duty is of my shift of deck watch, which occurred from midnight to 4:00 a.m. On watch, I had to make sure our ship kept its station in the convoy; it had to stay in line behind the ship in front of it. It wasn't the hardest work in the world, but I had to be awake—and alert. One night, all the ships coming in were completely blacked out so submarines couldn't spot us, and we were more than a thousand miles away from any light. The sky was like a kaleidoscope, ablaze with light shooting all over like the lighting at a Michael Jackson concert. It was truly unforgettable.

My ship became the first merchant ship to make it across the Atlantic in wartime without any escorts. I made two trips to England and one to the Mediterranean, where we unloaded fighter planes from our decks in Casablanca, Morocco. There were some harrowing moments. While our cargo of fuel was being unloaded. I was able to leave the ship and see some of Londo. I saw huge holes in the ground where German buzz bombs had hit, having wiped out entire city blocks. It seemed that the British people mainly slept in the subways. I can never forget how much damage and grief the war caused.

In one Italian port that had recently been liberated, we were lucky not to get blown up steaming ahead into a harbor full of mines that we were completely unaware of. Another time, we anchored at the British base at Gibraltar, on the southernmost point of Spain. The fascist government of Francisco Franco, who was sympathetic to Hitler, then controlled that country. Some Spaniards, pretending to be vendors selling stuff, would sneakily try to attach bombs to our ship's hull. I was issued a sidearm to guard against saboteurs. I warned the Spaniards to stop when they were approaching our ship in their small boats. They stopped because I had a gun in my hand. I didn't want to shoot and didn't have to.

After three round-trips across the Atlantic, I next sailed on a cargo ship through the Panama Canal—on the hottest day of my life—out into the Pacific as far as Hawaii. While docked in Honolulu, I ran into Herb Stein, a high school friend from Chattanooga who was in the navy. I invited him to come aboard my merchant ship for a meal in the officer's mess, where I was allowed to eat. Frankly, I was trying to show off, but the waiter refused to serve Herb. I asked why. He said under union rules, they wouldn't serve a visitor unless the ship's captain signed a chit for an hour of overtime. I said, "You're crazy; we're in a war."

The waiter said, "Our war is decades long."

The captain signed the chit, to my relief. The crew later told me the horrible history of the treatment of seamen, which included flogging and other cruel treatment. I began to understand why, even in wartime, the union's hard-earned gains were not to be waived.

We were scheduled to leave Honolulu and head for the Far Pacific, but at about that time, in April 1945, the war in Europe was ending, and for some reason, our ship returned to the West

Coast. We made port in San Francisco. I still remember the embarrassment of being refused a drink at the Top of the Mark bar at the Mark Hopkins Hotel despite my sea duty because I was only eighteen years old, while they served my twenty-one-year-old date. Then, when my sea duty ended there in San Francisco, I rode a dirty train home to Chattanooga and then to Great Neck, New York, and the Merchant Marine Academy.

I was a cadet at the Merchant Marine Academy when World War II ended in August 1945. We were released from duty on VJ Day, and we joined the wild crowd in New York City. We had the time of our lives, kissing girls and drinking beer. My buddy's wallet got stolen, so we were short on cash to pay our hotel bill. I wired my dad, who sent me the money to pay our bill.

I had my pretty uniform, but I didn't want to spend my life at sea. When the war was finally over in August 1945 and I was given the option to resign and go home a few weeks later, I accepted.

BACK TO SCHOOL

Without thinking of other schools or other careers, I automatically resumed working toward my engineering degree at Georgia Tech in the fall of 1945. I might add that, unlike all other veterans, those who served in the merchant marines were not legally given veteran status until decades later. I was thus not eligible for the GI Bill's financial support for my education. Although not well off, my father paid for my tuition and upkeep without any complaint.

Saying I had no talent in engineering doesn't begin to tell the whole story. I did fine with subjects that only required logic, but I had no mechanical aptitude and no depth perception. When I got to my junior year, I encountered a course in differential equations. I flunked it. But my true downfall came when I repeated the course and flunked it again. That automatically kicked me out of school.

Imagine my despair when I had to go home and tell my dad, who had saved money all his life to send me to college, that I had flunked out. To my everlasting relief, my dad was completely supportive and urged me to go back to Georgia Tech, point out that my other grades were good, and ask for another chance. I did, and they did give me another chance. What a difference a dad makes!

Despite being a veteran who had seen the world, I had a dismal social life at Georgia Tech in the postwar years. Tech was an all-male school, and everyone was in a hurry to catch up and finish school. Plus, I was still somewhat timid and insecure. I mostly dated high school girls who were more sophisticated than

I was. My routine consisted of classes and labs all week and then getting drunk on Saturday night.

I invited high school girlfriends from Chattanooga to visit me at Tech a few weekends. When my high school crush, Gerry Daneman, went to a fraternity party with me, sophisticated guys kept asking her to dance (she was really cute), and I felt left out. Also, I did have a short fling with a gal from the University of Georgia named Margaret Tepper, but she was definitely more advanced than I was, and soon, she drifted away to self-confident men.

There is one episode from my senior year at Georgia Tech that is certainly worth recalling. As I listened to the radio one afternoon, a broadcast from the University of Georgia, ninety miles away at Athens, announced names of students who had achieved scholastic honors. The names included Marianne Cohn. I remarked to Harry Baker, a frat brother standing nearby, "That girl is really cute. I can't believe she's smart too; that's really something. I remember seeing her at a party here, at our frat house, with one of our brothers, Lou Tipper."

Several days later, Harry Baker and I went to Athens to attend a sorority party. As I entered the sorority house, Marianne Cohn came rushing up to me and gave me a big hug, gushing about how sweet it was of me to send her a congratulatory telegram about her scholastic achievement. I looked at Harry standing next to me, grinning, and realized what he had done, and I played it cool. I'm not sure I ever told Marianne—who became my wife and the mother of our three children, nine grandchildren, and now one great-grandchild—that it was Harry, not me, who sent the wire.

My grades got worse as I progressed toward a degree in civil engineering, yet being a stubborn Capricorn, I persevered and graduated, barely. When my roommate and I finally knew for sure we were graduating from Georgia Tech, we sat down at a table in the frat house and consumed a fifth of whiskey each! I was still drunk when I got up the next morning. I then dug myself into a deeper hole by insisting on getting an engineering job, which I landed at—guess where?—the Tennessee Valley Authority (TVA).

My interest in Marianne Cohn did not end with my graduating from Georgia Tech in December 1948. It continued when I moved to Knoxville, Tennessee, for my first job as an engineer for TVA. We became engaged in 1949. I was very much in love. I married Marianne Cohn on January 22, 1950, when I was just twenty-four and she was only nineteen. She completed her college work at the University of Tennessee, majoring in English and graduating with honors.

The Graduate

My career as a civil engineer began at TVA working as a draftsman. I was a failure by any objective standards. I was not good at my work. I was passed over for promotions and was so aware of my shortcomings that I agreed with those decisions. My wife was the bright spot in my life in those years, when I knew I was failing at my job.

In my engineering experience, I did learn the value of details. If you spend months laying out the steel reinforcing bars in a power plant's thick, concrete floor slab, you do gain some respect for details. And being a loser for a few years taught me what it's like not to succeed, a lesson I did not always remember in dealing with people when I was on top in later years.

Looking back, I've realized that my engineering degree proves the basic point that all education is helpful, often in unexpected ways. For one thing, being an engineer mistakenly impressed people who hired me as a lawyer later, as well as those who worked for me. Perhaps most important of all, my degree taught me how most engineers think. Most engineers like certainty and believe politics and politicians are dirty. Engineers especially hate questions that imply criticism of the machines they design and build. That experience helped me manage utilities, which included lots of engineers.

A highlight of my married life was the birth of our first child, Anita, in 1954. She appeared angelic to me, the adoring father. I remember the anxiety that I felt the first day she came home from the hospital. My wife, Marianne; her mother, Suzanne; and I sat in the living room, waiting for something to happen. I would go into Anita's bedroom just to check on her every hour, even when she was sleeping peacefully; in other words, I was nervous and essentially useless.

Our second child, Stan, was born while I was going to law school in Knoxville, Tennessee. I recall sitting in a soft chair in Marianne's hospital room while she was giving birth in the delivery room. I was studying for exams, and of course, I fell asleep. I still remember the embarrassment I felt when Dr. Diddle, the OBGYN, gently tapped me on the shoulder to wake me up and said, "It's a boy."

My son Roger joined the family in 1959. All three of my kids were born in the East Tennessee Baptist Hospital in Knoxville.

BACK TO SCHOOL

I made my life-changing—really life-extending—decision when I was twenty-eight. I decided to quit engineering, go back to school, and sort of start over in a career—the most important decision I ever made. I knew I was no good as an engineer, but I had no idea what I wanted to study. I looked through the catalog for the University of Tennessee in Knoxville, where we lived, and found nothing that really turned me on.

But I made my decision. I had close friends on the TVA legal staff, Richard Freeman and Lee White, and I was jealous of them because the TVA lawyers had air-conditioned offices and we engineers didn't back in 1954. Also, they were meeting with my bosses, and I figured law must be a big deal. So I decided to try law school at the University of Tennessee, Knoxville. I started in 1954 after our first child, Anita, was born earlier that year, on March 6.

My father-in-law, a law school professor at the University of Georgia, advised me not to do it. He felt I wouldn't be able to support my family because lawyers earned so little in those days. I asked TVA to let me continue to work part-time as an engineer, and I received a reply from top management saying that they recruited their lawyers from Harvard and Yale and had no interest in my going to the University of Tennessee to become a lawyer. This really upset me, but the chief civil engineer, a very cultured European man named Adolph Meyer, promptly found a part-time job for me at TVA.

At school, I experienced great luck when Forest Lacey, the contracts professor at the University of Tennessee law school, gave a practice exam halfway through my first quarter. I got an F. I wrongly thought the point of an exam was to show your memory of the law, rather than to identify the legal issues raised by the question presented. I got the message loud and clear. I got an A on the real exam and would get almost straight As in all my classes, graduating first in my class. I had finally found something at which I excelled, really for the first time in my life, and a timid, insecure young man had turned into a cocksure know-it-all almost overnight.

My first big ego trip occurred when the TVA legal department offered me a part-time job when I was a senior in law school (before they hired me full-time after graduation). This was a far cry from TVA management's attitude when I first considered going to law school. My first assignment working part-time as a law school senior came from Charles McCarthy, then TVA's second-ranked attorney. He asked me to research whether TVA was subject to the federal income tax (FIT) law. Mind you, this was in 1956—TVA was twenty-three years old and had never filed a tax return, apparently because it was an exempt federally owned corporation.

I handed Mr. McCarthy a memo that concluded TVA was subject to the FIT law since the case law that opened it has no express exemption and everyone is subject to FIT. Mr. McCarthy read the memo and said, "Dave, this is an excellent piece of work. Please destroy all copies of this memo and forget that I ever asked you this question." I did what he asked, and even years later, when I was chairman of the TVA board of directors, I kept my word to Charles McCarthy and never mentioned the subject.

The University of Tennessee law school class sizes were small, only ten to fifteen students per class. I knew I was going to be called on in every class and thus had to be prepared by reading the assigned cases. I did not benefit from a super-bright student body, but I got the benefit of personally participating in every class. That would never have happened at Yale or Harvard, which I never considered attending.

The contrast between law education then and today's law education is striking. I needed only a college degree in any subject to gain admission to law school. I didn't need to take the SAT or any entry exam. And the class was 99 percent white males, with only one woman and one black man. One professor openly made sexually offensive comments about the woman without hesitation or reprimand. It was indeed a very different environment than today. Thank goodness it's different now.

Law school gave me a new life. I experienced the joy of learning and excelling. It instituted self-confidence that easily slipped into arrogance in later years, and it had unintended consequences in my relationship with my wife, explained by the saying "The law is a jealous mistress." My work competed for my attention and, over time, won out.

I have a vivid example of how a timid engineer turned into a superconfident troublemaker overnight. I was invited to be on the school's *Tennessee Law Review* in my first year. I completed my first case note two weeks before deadline so that, with my twenty hours a week of work at TVA, I would have enough time to make anticipated corrections. I heard nothing from the *Law Review* professor, Martin Ferrick, until the last day the case note was due, when he suggested numerous changes. I charged into his office and told him in blunt language that he had waited too long and he needed to make the changes himself. He did. And I became the class hero who told off the professor with a reputation for being arrogant.

I worked enough hours part-time at TVA to support my family while going to law school. I went to class straight through the summer, graduating in two and a half years. I was quite a busy guy. After I graduated from law school, much to my surprise, my best job offer came from the TVA legal department. I accepted because of the rich variety of legal work they offered and went to work full-time in January 1957.

DAVE THE LAWYER

My first boss as a lawyer was Joseph Swidler, TVA's general counsel. He had a talent for making a very mundane assignment seem like the most important thing on earth. He resigned about a year after I came on board, but we worked together long enough to know each other fairly well. In 1961, President Kennedy named Joe the chair of the Federal Power Commission (now the Federal Energy Regulatory Commission), and I later went to work for him.

As a TVA lawyer, for the first time in my life, I loved my work, and my work loved me. I handled a great variety of issues, ranging from power contracts and condemnation cases to appearances before the Interstate Commerce Commission (ICC) on freight rate cases. I also gained experience in human and corporate behavior that served me well later on in life.

One memorable experience I had as an attorney was when I defended TVA against a group of farmers. They lived near a TVA coal-fired power plant in East Tennessee. The farmers claimed the air pollution from the plant was killing the white pine trees on their farms. The TVA power people had planted some white pine trees in the Smoky Mountains as an experiment to show they, too, were dying, from regionwide bugs rather than pollution from the TVA power plants. As the TVA attorney, I thought that evidence looked good until I found out that white pines were dying around a similar coal plant in Pennsylvania. I then consulted with some scientists who told me the truth—that the emissions from the coal plant were indeed the reason the trees were dying. I never again trusted utility people on the issue of air pollution.

One of the cases assigned to me as a TVA lawyer was a complicated freight rate case before the ICC. I took over for Dick Freeman when he resigned to go work for the Chicago and North Western Railway, so the name Freeman still appeared on the papers TVA filed. The connection with Dick Freeman, then a TVA lawyer, was sort of prophetic. One day, as I walked down the hall in the ICC building, the ICC hearing examiner who was presiding over the case yelled, "My gosh, there really are two of you!" We, the two Freemans, created much more confusion and became the best of friends when we were together on the TVA board of directors many years later.

I was on the TVA legal staff from 1957 to 1961. I had a rich variety of work. A memorable case I handled was about the easement on certain land TVA needed to build a transmission line. TVA had apparently abandoned the easement, and someone had built a home on that land. TVA claimed that by law, the federal government couldn't abandon it's easement by not using it even for a very long time. TVA claimed the house was illegally located on TVA property and needed to be moved. I remember the homeowner's reaction like yesterday. When I knocked on his door to deliver the news, he grabbed a shotgun hanging on his wall, pointed it in my direction, and said, "You are Hitler. Get the hell out of my house!" I left.

I did some legwork and found out that the homeowner had bought the house at a bargain price because he knew it was on a TVA easement. Also, he owned the land right next to the easement, to which he could easily move the house, and that he did, after the federal judge ordered him off TVA property.

The people you meet along life's road are much more important than what you are working on. The TVA general counsel who first hired me, Joseph Swidler, turned out to be my ticket to the Kennedy administration. And the two people I first knew on the TVA legal staff, Lee White and Dick Freeman, played very important roles in my life.

OFF TO WASHINGTON, DC

In 1961, it was a big deal to get a job working for President Kennedy, and I got the fever. My good friend from his days at TVA, Lee White, was on President Kennedy's staff. He arranged for me to have a meeting with John Doar, who headed the Civil Rights Division at the Department of Justice. At the same time, Joe Swidler, my former boss at TVA, became the chairman of the Federal Power Commission (FPC) and offered me a job as his assistant. My interest in civil rights was intense, but my interest in energy was rather tame by contrast.

After the interview, Mr. Doar told me I was a fine young man and I would be a good addition to his staff but for one thing—my accent. He told me I couldn't win any case before a Southern jury because they would consider me a traitor to my Southern heritage. He said to take the FPC offer, which I did.

Marianne and I and our three children moved to Washington in the summer of 1961, and I began my career in energy as a second choice to one in civil rights, but still an exciting opportunity to be part of the Kennedy administration. I was thirty-five years old at the time, happily married with kids—Anita, aged seven; Stan, aged five; and Roger, aged two.

Moving from the South, we were pretty naïve about the ways of Washington, DC. I remember telling a real estate agent who showed us a house in Bethesda that I didn't want to live in a neighborhood that didn't welcome Jews, only to be told, "Well, I don't know if you are welcome in Bethesda, but about half of the people are Jewish!" Another surprise was that on a Sunday in Maryland in 1961, you couldn't buy alcohol or beer. In 1962, the home we bought in Bethesda, at 7211 Pyle Road, was nine miles from the White House and had a septic tank and well water. It only cost about thirty-five thousand dollars.

I plunged into my work at the FPC, but I was home with the family every evening and on weekends. I did bring work home but took time to read to the kids in the evening and play touch football with my sons and their friends on the weekend. And I did take my daughter, Anita, on her first dinner date.

Marianne was the active parent, and I was more like my kid's friend than their supervisory parent. Marianne gave up her career for many years to focus on raising the kids while I focused on my new career as a lawyer and public official. With the benefit of hindsight, I can see that my intense interest in my work began to drive an invisible wedge between Marianne and me. When I was an engineer, she was my sole focus. I was proud of Marianne when she went to Howard University in DC to get a master's degree in social work, but our interests diverged, and I was unaware that it was almost entirely our three kids keeping us together.

We were a nuclear family in which all our friendships were as a couple. The definition of *cheating* in my head was so rigid that I felt it improper to have a one-on-one lunch with a secretary. In fact, I had no women friends apart from our friends as a couple. In those days, people were just "by G—— married." They didn't ask themselves if they were happy.

At that time, I learned about my lack of sensitivity to black people. Having sat at a lunch counter with black people in protest, I had a heroic notion of my views on race, but I got a dose of reality when I told a joke with a racial slur in it to show my racial tolerance to the black secretary I had selected. I quickly realized what I had done and apologized to Norma Smith, my secretary, who said she assumed I was just another *white honky* she had to put up with.

Working directly for the FPC chairman, I had a chance to learn a lot. An early challenge was a huge backlog of natural gas pipeline rate cases. Chairman Swidler decided to settle them, and in the process, I had a chance to meet and get to know the top officers of the natural gas pipeline corporations. I had a similar experience with the electric utility leaders who participated in the FPC National Power Survey that planned the future of that industry for 1980.

Swidler taught me a lot by his example about not just holding office but actually pushing to get good things done. I also learned from his mistakes. I witnessed the importance of not running roughshod over your colleagues. He was the chairman, but he still needed three votes in the five-person FPC. He often failed to count to three, and when he did, he often didn't let the other two speak before they voted. The most glaring example was when he fired our chief administration officer one Saturday only to find out on Monday that he didn't have the authority to do so.

When Joe Swidler took over at the FPC, they actually had to track the path of electricity over interstate lines to assert jurisdiction over the wholesale rates of an electric utility—and that is virtually impossible. Chairman Swidler advanced the policy that if transmission lines crossed state lines, one could assume electricity flowed in interstate commerce and was subject to FPC jurisdiction. The U.S. Supreme Court agreed with the FPC in a 9–0 decision in a case involving the city of Colton, California. I attended the oral argument before the Supreme Court and recall Justice Black asking, "Who has got the burden of proof here? That side loses. It's like the rain dropping into a rain barrel—it just disappears."

In 1961, the FPC regulated the price of natural gas at wellheads. We faced a huge backlog of individual cases to be decided—well by well by well—one at a time. We consolidated them into area rate cases. The first one was the Permian Basin in Texas, where we fixed the price at eight cents per Mcf. Of course, that cost-based regulation was long ago repealed. Today, natural gas is considered cheap at three dollars per Mcf, which is quite a bit higher, even if you adjust for inflation.

When the FPC conducted a National Power Survey in 1963 and 1964, growth in electricity consumption was considered the best barometer for the growing strength of our economy. That was a time of Cold War with the Soviet Union. At one key meeting, FPC staff came up with a projection of US electricity consumption in 1980 that was lower than what the Soviet Union was projecting for 1980. Chairman Swidler said, "No, we are not going to let the Soviets beat us—give us a higher projection." And they did. *Efficiency* was not yet in the electric power industry's vocabulary, and not in mine either. It was also a time when nuclear power was considered the new clean and safe alternative to dirty coal. (Some folks still do.)

Joe Swidler taught me integrity by example. The FPC had a case pending in which the U.S. government was seeking a license to build a dam in Nevada. FPC rules forbade Chairman Swidler from having private communications with anyone about the case. I personally saw him hang up the telephone on the chairman of the Senate Committee on Appropriations, Senator Cannon of Nevada, who called to urge approval. And I also know Chairman Swidler refused to meet with Secretary of the Interior Udall to discuss the case.

I can't believe how politically naïve Joe Swidler and I both were. One day, Chairman Swidler's personal assistant got word from the White House that Ted Sorensen, President Kennedy's closest advisor, was reviewing the FPC's budget. I rushed into the chairman's office, saying, "The president must have something big in mind for us." Time went by, and nothing happened, so we figured it was just a rumor. At the same time, Chairman Swidler was refusing to meet with Secretary of the Interior Udall about the dam for which the Interior was seeking an FPC license. We never connected the two events.

It was only many years later that I read in a footnote in Ted Sorensen's book on the Kennedy presidency that he had held up the FPC budget to pressure Chairman Swidler to meet with Secretary Udall. Joe and I were too dumb politically to even realize we were being pressured!

One thing that grew during my four years at the FPC was my ego. On one of my first days at the FPC, I attended a ceremony with incoming chairman Joe Swidler where the outgoing chairman handed out awards and gave a medal to his personal assistant. With my then-pure, public-servant, self-effacing mindset, I said to Chairman Swidler, "I sure hope you never embarrass me with any such award." And when we left the FPC four years later, he followed my advice, and I received no tangible recognition. I remembered what I had said, but to be frank, I regretted it.

The 1961–1965 period was the heyday of the civil rights movement and included events such as the Cuban Missile Crisis. Energy was not a newsworthy issue, and the FPC didn't really get an inch of press until the day the lights went out, November 11, 1965, at 5:11 p.m. I happened to be alone in the chairman's office at that time, when all the phones started ringing at once. The lights had gone out all over the northeastern United States. Chairman Swidler had uncharacteristically left early. Our families had planned to have dessert together that night to discuss a request by President Johnson that day, asking Swidler to stay in office for the rest of the year, beyond the expiration of his term on November 30. Joe and I had planned to become law partners and had already rented space effective December 1, so we had a problem to discuss.

The blackout was a frightening event. President Johnson's first reaction was to call Secretary of Defense McNamara to make sure our missiles were alert—in the Cold War environment of the time, he suspected the Russians. His head of emergency management, General Browning, former governor of Tennessee, blamed a substation near Niagara Falls for causing the blackout, a statement that proved false.

I rounded up the other commissions, and Joe quickly returned to the office. Joe Califano, the president's aide, then called at 7:00 p.m. on behalf of the president and put the FPC in charge of getting the lights back on with the full power of the federal government at our disposal. We couldn't even get a phone call through to the Consolidated Edison Company at the center of the blackout area. No one knew what caused the blackout, and the nation remained frightened.

Fortunately, through a National Power Survey the FPC had underway, we knew the best experts in the electric power industry, and they were all summoned to Washington, DC, to meet the next morning. Swidler appeared on TV in the evening, saying, of all things, that blackouts could happen again. Soon thereafter, at 10:00 p.m., I got a call from Joe Califano telling me to get Chairman Swidler off of TV; he said, "He's scaring the hell out of folks, saying it could happen again."

I had the joy of delivering that message. Joe's reaction was "Well, you can't go on TV either." We designated one of our very knowledgeable and boring engineers, a Mr. Dean, for the job, and he put everyone to sleep with his technical jargon.

The next day, we pinned blame for the blackout on the Canadians' failure to maintain a transmission line going north from the Niagara Falls dam. The electric power industry faced the challenge of making the electric grid more reliable through technical changes.

After the FPC finally got some press, Joe Swidler and I left the FPC at the end of 1965 and formed the law firm of Swidler and Freeman. I frankly felt used in private practice because we were paid much for doing very little. My best friend, Lee White, was the new chairman of the FPC, and I suspected that our utility clients hired us because they thought we had influence, which we really didn't have.

Once, Lee invited my wife, Marianne, and I to join him and his wife, Dorothy, in Bethany Beach near Atlantic City for the weekend. Joe Swidler and I were representing Pacific Lighting at the time in a life-and-death fight with Tennessee Gas over the California market. The case was up for decision by the FPC, with Lee White having the crucial vote. I asked Lee if it was really wise for me to accept his invite. Lee replied that President Kennedy had once told him, "You can't really find new friends once you are in the office, so you've got to hold on to your old ones."

My client, Pacific Gas, said, "No, so don't go."

We rented a separate cabin but still had fun together and, of course, never talked business at all, except Lee joked, "The decision is in my briefcase." Today, it is just as important to look honest as it is to be honest, so we probably couldn't have that fun weekend now.

In private practice, Joe Swidler and I had plenty of clients, but the work posed no challenge for me or Joe, as compared to government service. After a few short years, with the help of my friend Lee White, I was back in government service.

WORKING IN THE WHITE HOUSE

In December 1967, when I was forty-one, President Johnson appointed me the first person in the American government with responsibility for energy policy. My job was to "coordinate energy policy on a governmentwide basis." To keep it out of politics, I was located in the president's science office under the science advisor. I had a two-person staff.

One of my first meetings in the White House with ordinary people gave me mind-blowing insight. In 1968, I knew a fair amount about energy, but the concept of efficiency in the end use of energy was about as remote to me as rocket science. Then two women from New Hampshire visited my office, and my conversation with them sent me on a new career path. They were opposed to a nuclear power plant near their homes and had done some research. They said that well-known efficiency measures, such as home insulation and more efficient lighting and refrigerators, could save more electricity than the nuclear power plant would produce. Furthermore, they claimed efficiency measures would be much cheaper than the nuclear plant and they could be installed in less than half the time required to build the plant.

I listened to them and examined their numbers, and as I did, I felt as if a light bulb, a very efficient one, went off in my head. I realized that energy efficiency wasn't just a big deal—it was a giant deal and needed to become a reality. I completed a governmentwide report in 1968, a plan for advanced siting of power plants so environmental concerns could be addressed before a site was selected. And in that report, the government raised the issue of energy efficiency for the first time. I believe this report, issued by the executive office of the president, was the first time the federal government called attention to and sought funding for research to address what we now call *climate change*.

The report drew the attention of a *New York Times* editorial on October 10, 1970. The editorial stated that the report "could hardly have made legislative recommendations more timely and sensible ... and calls for a degree of planning far greater than Americans have traditionally liked to think necessary."

I attended a sort of prophetic White House meeting in the spring of 1968 chaired by the budget director Charles Zwick. It was a big-picture meeting where energy, as a new subject, was on the agenda. I prepared a chart for the meeting that revealed almost all the federal research funding going to nuclear power at that time. There was zero funding for solar power and very little for coal research.

Before a large and influential audience, including my boss, the then science advisor Don Hornig, Mr. Zwick reacted to my chart rather decisively. He said, "Dave, I see your point, but I deal with agencies, not a subject such as energy. I can't take money away from Glenn [the chairman of the Atomic Energy Commission] and give it to Stuart [the secretary of the interior] and then tell Stuart that he must spend it on the sun rather than national parks." It was at that moment that the idea of the Department of Energy entered my head. President Nixon later formed the Energy Research and Development Administration, which then became the Department of Energy under President Carter, but I'm getting ahead of myself.

I left the big White House meeting pretty decisively rejected and dejected, as did everyone else in the room. I went back to my office and directed the National Science Foundation to award what was the first federal grant for research into solar power. The subsequent National Science Foundation report documented that solar hot-water heaters were economically feasible, especially if the technology was combined with solar cooling using the known technology that converted heat into refrigeration. It was a very small beginning.

I was really just getting started at trying to coordinate the government's energy activities under an "energy umbrella" when President Johnson announced in March 1968 that he was not running for reelection. And quite frankly, knowing he was going back home to Texas, he lost interest in the work I was undertaking, knowing that it would antagonize oil and gas interests.

Richard Nixon was elected in November 1968. I expected to leave office when he took office, so I was happy just to meet and say good-bye to Dr. Lee DuBridge, the ex-president of Caltech who was President Nixon's early appointed science advisor. To my shock, he said that he had discussed my work with President Nixon and he wanted to pursue it. Dr. DuBridge said he wanted me to stay on and lead it.

Being a Democrat in the Nixon administration's upper ranks was kind of like being a Jew in the very Christian South, where I grew up. I was special. I learned how hardball politics could be. The electric power industry sent a letter to President Nixon, questioning why I was still there.

Months later, a meeting was scheduled with utility leaders, and I was asked to chair the meeting. I said to John Ehrlichman, "Is this smart? You know those groups want me out of here."

He replied, "Dave, that's exactly why we want you to chair the meeting—they didn't contribute to the president's campaign."

A good example of the energy industry's state of mind in 1970 was a meeting I attended in the office of the then secretary of the interior, Rogers Morton. (Hickel had been let go by then.) The meeting was with the leaders of the electric power industry, and I was present to represent the White House and explain our power plant siting proposal, which included ideas for saving energy. An industry leader, the CEO of a North Carolina utility company, said to my face that my advocacy for energy efficiency was a Socialist thought—that in America, prosperity and the greater use of electricity went hand in hand. After the meeting, Secretary Morton said he then knew why utilities were not happy with the

Nixon administration—I was the problem. I didn't worry; John Ehrlichman had my back.

We published an important report titled "Electric Power and the Environment" in August 1970. In this report, we asked, "Do we really need all this added electric power?" and introduced energy efficiency into the policy discussion. But with the benefit of hindsight, another section of the report was perhaps even more important; it gave our recommendation for greater research funding for "broad long-range environmental questions."

In that report, we stated, "The principal questions involve the continental and global impact of projected emissions such as particulates, carbon dioxide, water vapor, and heat as well as the long-term effects of the chronic exposure of man and the web of plant and animal life to low-level radioactive and nonradioactive pollutants and to changes in temperature. One of the most complex issues involves the effects of simultaneous changes in particulates, carbon dioxide, and other emissions on the global weather" (p. 40).

I was given historic opportunities to participate in the environmental revolution that was underway during President Nixon's first term. My boss, Dr. DuBridge, was as kind and honest a man as I ever met. He allowed me to serve as staff to the Ash Council, a high-level group that was reorganizing the entire federal government. I wrote a memo proposing that we create an energy department and abolish the Atomic Energy Commission (AEC)—which had the conflicting jobs of promoting nuclear power while requiring expensive safeguards - and instead creating an independent nuclear regulatory agency. The idea gained a lot of attention, and the President Nixon residen discussed it with Representative Holifield of California, a strong supporter of nuclear power and chair of the Joint Committee on Atomic Energy. He was also chair of the House Government Operations Committee, which would have considered the legislation I had proposed. Mr. Holifield said no way, and the idea died then, but both agencies were enacted years later.

A more effective effort by the Ash Council resulted in the independent Environmental Protection Agency (EPA), created by President Nixon. Doug Costle (later an EPA head under President Carter) and I were the staff who actually lobbied the Ash Council to propose the EPA. The then secretary of the interior, Wally Hickel, adamantly claimed it should be a part of his agency. We were lucky that the president and his top staff didn't like Hickel much. (They later replaced him.) John Ehrlichman supported an independent EPA, and it was submitted to Congress under a statute that provided that the EPA would become law if Congress didn't vote no within thirty days. And the EPA did become law.

I had the privilege of being present at the creation of the Clean Water Act, the Air Quality Act, the National Environmental Policy Act, and the National Environmental Council, all created under President Nixon's leadership. This was the golden age of the environmental movement; President Nixon would be called an environmental extremist by twenty-first-century standards.

John Ehrlichman deserves major credit for making it all happen. Ehrlichman, an environmental lawyer from Seattle, was delegated full control by President Nixon, who simply said to Ehrlichman, "We probably will be running in 1972 against Senator Muskie from Maine, a strong environmentalist, and I want to have a good environmental record." The rest is history.

It is useful to recall that forty-five years ago—before we even recognized the awesome threat of climate change—America was united in the need to pass laws to control pollution. Republicans and Democrats competed for getting the credit for laws to clean our air and water, and a Republican president, Democratic leaders, and Congress worked together to pass the necessary laws.

Today, in addition to the debilitating impact of partisan polluters, we face a pollution problem unlike dirty air and polluted water—climate change, a problem that is scientifically certain but one that the ordinary human cannot see. We are behaving like the animals that have a sense of smell and sight but no brainpower. But what good are our brains if we don't use them? That is the problem with controlling climate change—it is out of sight, a sad commentary on so-called educated human beings.

Working in the White House's science office under two very different presidents enabled me to gain valuable insight into the role of science in making government policy, and also insight into what I call the *self-serving interest of the science community.* The fact that permanent scientists, with scientific facts on their side, were able to shut down the supersonic airplane against the president's wishes is a testament to their potential clout. We are today witnessing the same strength trying valiantly to set combat climate change in an era when the people are much less inclined to listen to reason.

Also, I learned that scientists are most interested in persuading the most challenging technical options at the expense of solutions that could be more easily achieved. A good example is scientists' sixty-year romance with fusion power to duplicate the sun's heat in order to make electricity, rather than advance more mundane solar, wind, and storage technologies, which have finally turned commercial.

Every year I worked in the White House's science office, the scientists at Princeton lobbied me, and others, very successfully that they needed more money for fusion research—that success was at hand. President Nixon sent the first energy message to Congress in 1971. I had the job of coordinating the sometimes-conflicting views of all the government agencies and drafting the message.

At an initial defining meeting, the major agencies debated whether our goal was an abundant supply of energy—as many of the statutes from the 1930s required—or, as I suggested, an adequate supply. Everyone in the room who spoke up, especially John Nassikas, the chairman of the FPC, favored *abundant*. I made the pitch for efficiency and said using *adequate* would begin to make efficiency part of the energy policy. The debate continued, and finally, John Whitaker, an aide to Ehrlichman, said, "Dave's drafting this message, and he wins this one. Let's move on."

That rather abstract decision may very well have been the first time energy efficiency was recognized as part of national energy policy. The message did include the first real action to advance efficiency. It ordered the Federal Housing Authority to require insulation standards in Federal Housing Authority loan-approved homes.

I must admit the message also promoted the nuclear breeder reactor, which was the centerpiece of nuclear power that was then considered the "clean," superabundant source of our energy future. The promotion of the nuclear breeder was one item decided by President Nixon himself. I was present at the meeting the president chaired to make that decision. He was quite well prepared. At one point, he asked the AEC chairman, Glenn Seaborg, "Don't we have another SST on our hands?" The SST (supersonic transport) was the superplane that many scientists believed threatened the environment. Congress had defeated it, despite President Nixon's support.

Seaborg answered, "No, Mr. President. No such problem."

President Nixon paused, ignored Seaborg's answer, and said, "Well, we're going to go ahead anyhow." The breeder reactor turned out to be a technological turkey, which, seventeen years later, I played a decisive role in putting to death.

The only time I had what you might call a *personal meeting* with President Nixon was one Saturday morning in 1970. I took my son Stan with me to work in the White House that day. As we finished up, John Whitaker, the top guy under Ehrlichman, said, "The president is about to leave for Camp David. Let's go catch him and let Stan meet him."

I asked, "Can I go too?" and he said of course.

We chatted briefly with the president just outside the Oval Office as he headed for his helicopter. He did shake hands with Stan, after which Whitaker later said to me, "I bet Stan will vote Democrat anyhow." And he has.

The most important energy policy issue the Nixon administration addressed in depth was the danger of America's dependence on oil imports from the Middle East. Dr. DuBridge allowed me to serve in his place on a task force President Nixon created to study the oil import issue, a concern that has since plagued the country for forty years. George Shultz, the then secretary of labor, chaired the task force, instead of Wally Hickel, the secretary of the interior—the agency that managed the then existing program of import control—because the president just didn't trust Hickel.

It's useful to recall that beginning with the Eisenhower administration in the early 1950s, America had strict quotas that controlled the amount of petroleum that could get imported. This protected the domestic petroleum industry from the competition of lower-priced oil on the world market. These import controls, combined with limits on production imposed by the Texas and Louisiana state governments, were designed to prop up the price of American-produced oil. And of course the depletion allowance enabled the petroleum industry to avoid much of their tax burden. The petroleum industry pretty much dictated America's energy policy. We also used to joke that our basic policy was "to pray for mild weather."

By 1971, the oil import controls had become an unmanageable problem, and the study was ordered to find a better policy. Highly skilled professionals conducted the study. The final report concluded that America had a serious national security problem if imports from outside the Western Hemisphere exceeded 10 percent. The report drew serious opposition from the major oil companies, who were beginning to import more and more of their oil.

President Nixon failed to approve the report's recommendations because he felt that supporting the report against oil industry opposition would harm the race of George H. W. Bush, who was running for Congress in Texas. This episode demonstrated the integrity of then secretary of state George Shultz, who persuaded the president to release the report to the public so that he, George Shultz, could remain silent on the subject.

My most personally important meeting I had in the nearly four years I served in the White House's science office was the one I had with John Ehrlichman in the spring of 1971. He said to me, "If you have any more good ideas, let's hear them right now, because we're going 100 percent political from now on. If I were you, I'd get the hell out of here. The 'old man' isn't ever going to appoint you to any big job because you are a Democrat. Leave now, and if Muskie wins, you can come back and do some good." That was the best vocational guidance I ever got, and I took it by resigning in June 1971.

MY PERSONAL LIFE

Marianne and I were into our twentieth year as a married couple. Without our realizing it at the time, our interests had continuously diverged. I was loving my work more than my wife, even though we were a completely faithful couple that got along well on the surface. She gained her master's degree in social work and worked for the DC city council. She was successful in her work but did not feel the same degree of satisfaction in work that I was achieving. We did not share our important thoughts, and unspoken resentments started to build up.

The celebration of my son Stan's bar mitzvah in late 1969 was a memorable event for me. We had a dinner party at the National Press Club in Washington, DC. Since I worked in the White House, a number of notables attended. But the speeches that stirred the audience came from my dad and Marianne's dad. Both of them could speak to the freedoms they enjoyed as Americans as people who knew the difference between the United States and Nazi Germany and Communist Russia.

As it happened, this happy event was the last time my dad was his vigorous self, holding an audience of big shots entranced with his heartfelt love of America. In 1970, my dad became quite ill at age eighty-five and after a battle with cancer passed away from a sudden heart attack. I did have the good fortune of spending sizable blocks of time at his bedside while he was still very much with it. I have a clear recollection of one conversation that made a lasting impression on me. I bragged to him about having played a role in the congressional enactment of a coal mine safety bill after a terrible disaster in Farmington, West Virginia. He let me explain in detail how *great* we were in getting this bill passed that would strengthen coal mine safety standards. He then asked me one simple question: "Will they enforce it?" That one question cut to the heart of things and helped me focus on achieving results in later years.

My dad gave me another gift when I bragged to him about working in the White House. He said, "You are only forty-four, and you are going to do a whole lot bigger things than that." I didn't appreciate his 100 percent faith and belief in me very much at the time, but it actually provided inspiration and support during rough times in the future.

My dad was the son of a Lithuanian rabbi who sent him to the famous Slabotsky Yeshira to learn about the Jewish religion. His family was very poor, and my dad got his meals at the homes of nearby Jews. Each night, he ate potatoes, to the point that he sang me a little song about it in Yiddish, "Montag bulbes. Dienstag bulbes, Mitworth nach agin bulbes"—which meant Monday, potatoes; Tuesday, potatoes; Wednesday, once more, potatoes.

In his last days, my dad kept reiterating his faith in America. He told me that someday a Jew would become president, and then he said yes, someday we would have a black man as president. But his important last gift to me was his philosophy of life. My dad said life boils down to just two things: The first part is that life should be joyous; no matter your situation, look for the happy side of things. Life itself is a joy, not a tragedy, so live it that way. The second part is that life is a contact sport, and unless you stand for something bigger than yourself and fight and struggle for it, you're not living—just drifting, existing, and floating through life. These two fundamental ideas—that life is a joyous struggle and you must live as a happy warrior—have served me well, and I thank my dad for giving me this insightful map for life's road.

Teaching and Writing

I spent the year after leaving the White House as the Alcoa visiting professor at the University of Pittsburgh while writing a book. I continued to live in DC and flew to Pittsburgh on Monday mornings and returned on Thursdays. I taught a class on energy policy and organized a master's program on energy. I discovered that getting agreement among professors was no different than in any large organization—anything new was threatening. The fact that I was only there for a year and didn't create a position for myself was the main reason I got the program done.

I found that teaching and writing a book was a great combination. I could test my energy policy ideas with my class, which gave me tremendous feedback for my book. I suggested calling my book *The Joyride Is Over*, but my publisher said negative titles don't sell, and we ended up with *Energy: The New Era*, which still didn't become a best seller. It was published in 1973. I did get pleasure from learning that the reading list for a class my son Stan took at the University of Michigan included my book.

The Twentieth Century Fund originally agreed to sponsor my book with a sizable bonus if they approved of its contents. However, the fund's executive director objected very strongly to the last chapter, which raised the fundamental conflict posed by our enormous appetite for material affluence destroying our environment. I raised the question "How much is enough?" and pointed out the dire threat that per capita energy consumption in America posed to the planet. I suggested ideas to move to a more durable society than the throwaway society caused by the material affluence that we kept enlarging. I was bluntly told to drop this last chapter or else the Twentieth Century Fund would not endorse my book or give me a bonus. I didn't drop the last chapter and got no bonus or any help in getting a publisher. I do feel some pride that Random House ended up publishing the book in paperback after some obscure outfit published a hardcover version.

As I reread my book, I find that I really haven't learned much in the last forty years. My views on energy and the environment were pretty well formed when I wrote the book in 1972 and 1973, and they are as relevant in 2016 as they were then. For example, I said:

"The most important reality is that America has been devouring energy as though it were as plentiful as water in a rainstorm" (p. 7).

"A national policy of conserving energy would constitute a sharp break from the past in the U.S. But such a policy is no longer an option; it is a necessity" (p. 299).

"All the theories about the effects of carbon dioxide and particulate matter buildup are speculative. The fact is we simply do not know what will happen. We can only be certain that man is tampering ignorantly and perhaps dangerously with the planet's environment in a very fundamental way. And If we find that excessive fuel consumption is causing threatening changes in climate, the lead time for reducing fuel consumption to ward off the threat will be quite short. The effects on a high-energy civilization without alternatives could be disastrous" (pp. 50–51).

"The future of mankind requires the development of renewable sources of energy. Only then will it be possible to aspire to an improving quality of life and flourishing civilization into the distant future" (p. 339).

One of the numerous important breaks in my career came in 1972 when Gordon Hamilton and Ned Ames of the Ford Foundation approached me about leading a major energy policy study. They were both environmentally sensitive and interested in making sure the study gave energy conservation a fair shake. The study was unique for the Ford Foundation. Rather than giving a grant to an existing organization, such as Resources for the

Future, which Ford already funded, they wanted a fresh look at the energy issue. They hired me to recruit a staff and work directly for the Ford Foundation. The pay was not great, but that Ford Foundation credit card was fabulous.

The study started and ended with controversy. I negotiated a deal with the foundation that gave me the final word on what the study would conclude and complete control of the staff I recruited. I did agree to work under a broad-based advisory board and to include board members' comments, along with the study's conclusions, in the final report. But the agreement made it clear that the advisory board would just advise and I would decide what the study concluded.

The first controversy hung over me before I was even hired. Industry friends of Henry Ford III felt concerned, with justification, that I would advance my views on the role of efficiency, which they considered a threat. They scheduled a meeting before the entire Ford Foundation board of directors, which included Mr. Ford, McGeorge Bundy, Robert McNamara, and other big names. Mr. Ford actually asked me, "What do you think of the automobile?" So help me, he did ask me that. I said I owned two of them and loved them but spent a fair amount of time at the filling station getting repairs done. Mr. Ford's questions went on. "Do you have an open mind?" he asked.

I said, "Yes, I have an open mind but not an empty one. Look around you, Mr. Ford. We are in an essentially glass house. [The Ford Foundation headquarters in New York City had largely glass walls.] You keep the temperature some twenty to forty degrees cooler or warmer than it is outdoors, with virtually no shelter from the building itself. We are wasting energy that could be conserved, and that will be a part of our study." There were no more questions, and I did get the job.

My first decision was *not* to hire any energy experts but rather smart, young people with open minds. And that's what I did. We also awarded grants to independent professionals for specific pieces of work.

One of the most interesting studies we did was completed by Mason Willrich, a University of Virginia professor. His research revealed it was possible to design an atomic bomb from information available at a public library. Obviously, terrorists can use public libraries, and our study revealed that fact in order to alarm the government that they should become concerned about loose nukes. To publish any study, we needed approval from McGeorge Bundy, the head of the Ford Foundation and former national security advisor to President Kennedy. During a conversation on a Friday afternoon, Mr. Bundy suggested that I must be joking, asking that he approve a "cookbook on how to make a bomb."

I said, "Mr. Bundy, please just think about it over the weekend, and then let me know." He did and said okay on Monday morning, realizing the information was out there—and that the nation needed to start safeguarding against that threat. The publication played its intended role back in 1973. The AEC began to take much more seriously the problem of nuclear proliferation.

The Energy Policy Project, as we called it, sponsored studies on energy subjects as far-ranging as oil spill protection and nuclear safety. In total, the Ford Foundation invested about $4 million for the staff work and the studies we approved—a sizable sum in the early 1970s. The publication that got the widest exposure was a preliminary report we published and distributed in 1973 during the oil embargo. The book of the month club distributed about four hundred thousand free copies to customers who bought other books.

The Energy Policy Project, located in Washington, DC, was hot during the oil embargo of 1973 as a knowledgeable, impartial source of information about energy. We made more than twenty appearances before committees of Congress and briefed important members of the press. Perhaps my most useful appearance was as the invited guest of the National Governors Conference on June 5, 1973. There were only two guests, me and Frank Ikard, the head of the American Petroleum Institute. Among the governors participating were two future presidents—Jimmy

Carter and Ronald Reagan. Governor Carter and I had a personal, friendly exchange, the record reveals. That was the first time he heard me speak. I recall him saying he had just been to Israel, and I wondered if that Georgia governor didn't have higher ambitions.

I delivered a strong pitch for energy efficiency at the conference, some forty-three years ago. It was probably the first time those governors were exposed to a serious presentation of that idea. I told them, "Energy conservation is no longer just a desirable option. It is an absolute necessity. We have to do a lot more than just pay lip service to it. We can get by with a lot less growth in energy consumption because a lot of what is used goes out the window, up the stack, and out of the exhaust pipes in our cars. No one would think of throwing money out of the window but that is what most of us do every day as we overheat glass buildings in the winter and overcool them in the summer" (p. 54).

I also spoke strongly in 1973 about the need to protect the environment, a need that is just as relevant today, as follows:

> America stands at a crossroads in facing the energy problems. Certainly, we ignore the current shortages at our peril. But I think there is a graver danger in pushing the panic button and turning our back on the progress we have made in the last few years in cleaning up the environment. Let us not forget for a moment that it is the production of energy that is polluting the air in our cities and endangering human health. After all, we are the trustees for future generations in protecting the basic resources for which the nation has been so abundantly endorsed. Let's begin by measuring our progress by the quality of what we leave behind rather than how much we burn and devour.

The governors were attentive and asked lots of good questions.

A speech I made before the Consumer Federation of America during the oil embargo got me into hot water. I was in big trouble because I did not have a disclaimer in my text saying I was just speaking for myself, not the Ford Foundation. I'd like to say it was an oversight, but I actually considered a disclaimer and decided not to insert it because I thought nobody would care. Well, someone did care—William Tavoulareas, the CEO of Mobil Oil, who was on our advisory board. Not only did he want me fired, but the Ford Foundation worried that I was endangering their status as a tax-free organization.

The speech caused quite a ruckus because Walter Cronkite quoted it on the *CBS Evening News*: "The energy crisis is a smokescreen for the petroleum industry to pick the pockets of the American people to the tune of billions of dollars." Not exactly an evenhanded analysis of the situation, but in my mind, it was an essentially true statement. I didn't get fired, primarily because firing me would have made the Ford Foundation appear in cahoots with the oil industry, in which the foundation had significant investments.

While I had negotiated for control of my staff and the content of our final report, I still needed the Ford Foundation's approval of all grants and other expenditures. Ordinarily, that would be a laborious and lengthy process, as we were located in Washington, DC, and the Ford Foundation was in New York City, but we had friends in court, so to speak, in Ned Ames and Bobbi McKellar, who expedited our requests and approved our lavish expense accounts. Imagine an evening in New York City with a Ford Foundation credit card!

An experience that did not sink in until years later was how Marianne, my wife, reacted when she once stopped by to see me while I worked with my staff on the Energy Policy Project. We were intensively working to complete our report. It hit me that my activities were new to her as she expressed surprise at and admiration for my work. It was a compliment that also revealed how we were apart, except for our interactions with our kids and friends of our nuclear family.

As part of my agreement with the Ford Foundation, they paid for my first visit to Israel, which I was planning to make when they recruited me. My mother, Lena, and my son Roger, who was then fourteen, accompanied me. Marianne decided not to go along even though I wanted her to come.

We arrived right after the 1973 war ended. I was the guest of Uri Marinov, head of the Israeli Environmental Agency. He arranged for me and my family to go up to the Golan Heights. We were driven along the road that was the boundary with Syria. We saw Syrian soldiers with guns in their hands staring at us only a few days after the war had ended. This made a lasting impression of how controlling those heights could lead to control of so much of Israel.

A first trip to Israel is always impressive, but we received superb treatment as special guests. My mother was especially thrilled because the trip fulfilled a dream for her. And despite her age, she had no trouble keeping up with the rest of us.

While there, I did learn of Israel's history with nuclear power. I asked why they were even considering a nuclear power plant, and they said their first leader, David Ben-Gurion, said that Israel couldn't be a modern nation without nuclear power. I believe I did help convince the government leaders with whom I spoke that a nuclear plant in Israel would be a radioactive Trojan horse that would give neighboring nations claims to nuclear plants of their own. And of course, a nuclear power plant is the path to building a bomb.

I met Israeli solar power researchers, but unfortunately, they weren't getting much support from an Israeli government preoccupied with war and security. Back in 1973, Israel was switching its electric power plants from oil to coal. Relying on Arab oil was a huge concern. Coal from friendly South Africa was their solution.

As we began preparing the final report of the Ford Foundation Energy Policy Project based on the extensive research we commissioned, I learned a lot about teamwork and how to make it happen. My team members were all going to lose their jobs when the study concluded. My influence as their boss disappeared by the day. I decided to give everyone a piece of the action—the entire staff had to agree on the wording of the final report. The staff took that as a vote of confidence; it turned out to be a terrific unifying approach. Even so, the lesson of the importance of delegation and giving the whole team some skin in the game did not really sink in until much later in my career.

When we released our final report, titled "A Time to Choose," in October 1974, we received an unexpected barrage of publicity. My nemesis, Mr. Tavoulareas, the CEO of Mobil Oil, was enraged by our conclusions that established energy efficiency as a major source of clean energy and focused on the pollution caused by fossil fuels. Mobil Oil bought large advertisements in the *New York Times* and *Washington Post* blasting our findings to high heaven. These ads brought more attention to our report than any PR campaign we could have launched. Our message on energy efficiency did sink into the energy policy debate, and to an extent, it would never have done so without the oil industry's opposition.

We did publish the comments by Mr. Tavoulareas and other advisory board members in our report, along with our findings, as we promised. When I look back on the industry's comments on "A Time to Choose," they reveal just how groundbreaking and prophetic we were. They also reveal how much progress America has made in advancing energy efficiency and environmental protection. In an article about me on September 27, 1992, the *New York Times* observed that at the time, in 1974, oil and utilities companies said, "My idea [efficiency] was radical and wrong, but in fact it wasn't radical enough."

The media coverage for "A Time to Choose" was only the most visible part of its impact. I decided to mail a copy of the report to the governor of each state, and thus, a copy was sent to Governor Jimmy Carter of Georgia. According to Ami Walden, who was then Governor Carter's staff person on energy, he handed her his copy of "A Time to Choose" and asked her to read it and write an executive summary. She noticed that some pages had been torn out of the beginning of her copy but read it and prepared a summary of what she had read. After reading her summary, Governor Carter said, "I only read their summary and pretty much agreed with it but wanted to be sure the report really supports their summary. Your summary is about the same as theirs, so I'm satisfied they can back up their findings. You can use this report as a guide for my own energy policy." I, of course, had no idea that any of the governors to whom I sent "A Time to Choose" would ever become president of the United States, but this episode reveals that sometimes, you make your own luck.

The CEO of Mobil Oil did not fade away. He continued to complain to the Ford Foundation that our report was not supported by research, that it was just a personal, radical pitch by me. To settle the issue once and for all, the Ford Foundation printed his complaints once more in 1977, together with a reply by Carl Kaysen, a respected economist at Princeton. Mr. Kaysen concluded that "A Time to Choose" was "a timely and useful book which performed a real service by helping to make energy conservation a respectable subject for analysis and policy."

By then, President Carter had embraced the report's major thesis—efficiency—as the heart of his energy policy.

ON TO CAPITOL HILL

My next move after completing "A Time to Choose" was to work on Capitol Hill to try to implement the conservation options we identified in the report. Based on a friendship developed years before with Mike Pertschuk, chief of staff of the Senate Commerce Committee that the senator Warren Magnuson chaired, I was hired to work for that committee. I remember my first sit-down meeting with Mike and Lynn Sutcliffe, the general council of the committee. They asked me what the most important recommendation in "A Time to Choose" was, and I said a law to require improved automobile efficiency. And that was the moment in 1974 when the idea of what we now call *CAFE* (Corporate Average Fuel Economy) was born.

We drafted a bill and persuaded Senator Hollings of South Carolina, then a fairly junior senator, to sponsor the legislation and to chair the hearings approved by Chairman Magnuson. A young science intern on the staff named Allan Hoffman did all the hard work of drafting the bill and pulling together the relevant facts. Then we were underway. In 1974, memory of the recent oil embargo was still strong, so we were optimistic.

The president at that time was Gerald Ford from Michigan, the home of the auto industry. He did not support the bill, and his agencies were not helpful. We gathered the factual support for the bill "by hook or by crook." One source was a young staffer at the Federal Energy Administration (FEA) named Robert Hemphill, who brought us information after work on his motorbike. I believe a chance to visit one of Senator Hollings's very attractive Southern belles might have been an effective incentive for him to help.

We also got support from prominent celebrities, such as Robert Redford, who had enormous influence over male members of Congress who loved to drop his name to female friends. Bob's huge strength as a salesman of CAFE standards was that he personally visited members of Congress, and when he did, he knew the subject matter better than they did.

At the 1974 hearing on the CAFE standards bill, the Ford administration witnesses said that they had letters from top auto executives agreeing to improve automobile fuel efficiency in the years ahead and that no legislation was needed because they were "honorable men." Senator Hollings pointed out that the auto companies did not oppose similar legislation imposing mandatory insulation standards for houses. "Is it your opinion," asked Senator Hollings, "that housing executives are 'dishonorable men'?" The bill passed the committee but did not become law in 1974.

In 1975, we saw another opportunity. The legislation for the FEA was up for renewal, and the Ford administration wanted it renewed. We planned to add the CAFE standards as an amendment to the FEA renewal bill. Commerce Committee Chairman Magnuson permitted me to work with any senator interested in energy, and we persuaded Senator Ted Kennedy to agree to lead this renewed effort to enact the CAFE standards into law.

Attaching the CAFE standards to the FEA extension bill was no problem in the Senate, where it passed smoothly, but getting it through the House side was tough. The Ford administration lobbied hard to block the CAFE standards. Two people made it happen. First, Senator Kennedy's personal clout helped, especially with the House speaker, Tip O'Neill, from his home state of Massachusetts. I heard him jokingly tell Tip he would leave him out of his cabinet if he didn't get the CAFE standards passed. Remember, this was 1975, well before the Chappaquiddick incident clouded Senator Kennedy's chances to become president.

No one really knew the breadth of Senator Kennedy's role in the Senate. At one point in the CAFE standard fight, we needed to persuade a western senator. Senator Kennedy just said, "No,

Indians, Bobby." He was silently carrying out his dead brother's agenda. Edward Kennedy was by far the most organized, hard-working, and effective senator I observed while working directly with a fair number as a staffer. He told me to walk into his office whenever I needed him to do anything, no matter what. He always made any call I asked.

Ted Kennedy is primarily responsible for Congress's final passage of the CAFE standards. Yet he accomplished so much more that he never got any public credit for. But he didn't forget. Thirty years later, at a 2004 fundraiser for Senator Kerry in DC, he spotted me across the large room, called me over, and joked with Kerry that he, and I, had passed the bill, so why couldn't he, Kerry, up the ante?

The other person responsible was Robert Redford, who personally spoke to key congressmen in favor of the bill and offered his support to a key House Committee chairman. Redford actually agreed to appear for him in his district to overcome the Ford administration's lobbying against the bill. And Bob kept his word and appeared in the chairman's Ohio district to help him get reelected.

In 1974 and 1975, the Senate Commerce Committee was a beehive of consumer and environmental legislation. In addition to the CAFE standards, one of the earliest pieces of energy legislation was the "Truth in Labeling" Act sponsored by Senator Tunney. I testified in support of the bill even though I was a staffer. It required energy-intensive appliances—such as air conditioners, washers, dryers, and refrigerators—to have labels that clearly stated just how much electricity they would consume. This law, which is still enforced today, requires easy-to-read information so consumers can shop for the most efficient appliances.

The influence of Chairman Magnuson's Senate Commerce Committee was so great in 1975 that the mere introduction of legislation by it could trigger change in the real world; for example, committee staff (me) felt a great need for more research into cleaner and more efficient technology for generating and transmitting electricity. The industry was investing very little at the time, so Senator Magnuson introduced a bill to levy a 1 percent tax on electricity, with the funds given to electric power research. The bill was never enacted because it helped the industry establish and fund its own Electric Power Research Institute, which continues to function forty years later.

I was privileged to get to work with a number of senators while on the Commerce Committee staff. One meeting with Senator Mondale had a lasting impression on me. We discussed the idea of increasing the tax on gasoline to encourage people to buy more efficient automobiles. Mondale was emphatic—he would never vote to increase the price of gasoline, ever. It was a tax on something essential to most folks. He just wouldn't. He would have rather attacked the oil companies if they raised the price.

It turned out he was right about Congress's chosen approach. Over a fifty-year period—whether it was a BTU tax, cap and trade, or a carbon tax—the answer from Congress on raising the price of energy, by whatever name, has been "Hell no!"

A Personal Note

I recall driving home one night in the summer of 1976 and remarking to Marianne that I was getting really excited by having a candidate for president, Jimmy Carter, advocating energy policies and sounding a lot like me. I said, "If he runs, I sure look forward to joining his administration." I then remember being disappointed by her reaction, that she thought we ought to be spending more time with family and planning for retirement. I was barely fifty years old; I received this as a clear signal that we were growing apart, not together, and indeed were in wholly different worlds, bound only by three kids, aged twenty-two, twenty, and seventeen.

In 1976, I listened with growing delight to Governor Carter's statements on energy as he campaigned for president. As the summer progressed, my delight with Jimmy Carter began to turn to disappointment as Carter kept expressing views that reflected "A Time to Choose" without inviting me to join his policy team in Atlanta, or his campaign. Finally, I called a friend, Joe Browder, who was a member of the Carter policy team in Atlanta. He invited me to stop by during my August vacation. I did not realize on arrival that I was crashing the party, so to speak.

MY RENDEZVOUS WITH JIMMY CARTER

Upon arriving in Atlanta in late August 1976, I quickly got involved in the work of preparing policy papers for use if Governor Carter was elected president. After I got involved, I had no intention of stopping, and I appeared welcome. And for the first time in a then twenty-six-year marriage, I became unemployed. I quit my job with the Senate Commerce Committee and worked for nothing as a volunteer for Jimmy Carter. I don't recall showing Marianne the respect and courtesy of discussing it with her before informing her of my decision. I was so excited about the opportunity that I did not even recognize that this was a major step toward the end of our nuclear family.

I was still at a loss of how I had crashed the party when Frank Moore, Governor Carter's finance man, stopped by my desk one day after I'd been at the job for a month and asked me not to attend a meeting between Governor Carter and a group of the nation's leading energy executives that I had set up. To my almost-screaming question of "Why not?" he calmly told me that in exchange for a badly needed seventy-thousand-dollar contribution from the oil industry some months before, he had promised that neither Lee White, former FPC chair, nor I would be part of the Carter administration.

I then asked, "Does Governor Carter know about this?"

Frank said, "Oh Lord, *no*. If he did, he'd fire me."

I then said, "Frank, we have a problem."

We sat down with Jack Watson, the head of the policy team, and all three of us agreed that Frank's promise was dead and that I was now a full member of the team. Given the circumstances, I decided not to go to the energy meeting, and Frank, who became the president's liaison to Congress, was forever grateful.

After such a unique entrance into the Carter team, I was quite well received. I wrote the energy policy paper that focused on tax reform, which was a presidential priority. My paper proposed reducing income taxes and replacing the revenues with higher taxes on gasoline. Just as Senator Mondale, then vice president, had predicted, it was politically dead on arrival. Also, I played a significant role during the transition in suggesting Jim Schlesinger be energy secretary, as an alternative to his being secretary of defense, as some of the Carter advisors feared. I knew Jim from our times together in the Nixon administration and helped assure him that he was uniquely qualified for the job.

I spent several months working on policy papers that would be important if Governor Carter won but useless if he lost. It was an interesting time for me. My morale went up and down with the polls. On the Friday before the election the next Tuesday, Gerald Ford pulled slightly ahead. To shrug off the feelings of depression, I must admit that a fellow policy paper workmate, Kathy Fletcher, and I went shopping. Despite all my ranting about how buying too much stuff would ruin the environment, I resorted to the very weakness I preached against. But lo and behold, Candidate Carter was the comeback kid. At 4:00 a.m. the morning after the election, the vote in Mississippi sealed his victory.

The election of Jimmy Carter as president, as a practical matter, marked the end of my marriage to Marianne. We did not get divorced until 1980, but it was more than symbolic that while she visited me in Atlanta, she was not with me when I was one of the first people to shake the new president's hand at 4:00 a.m. after he declared victory. That was by no means her fault. I was more interested in being with the people I had worked with on the campaign. I then moved back home to Washington, DC, for the transition months before Governor Carter took office in January. But I was at home pretty much only to sleep.

I was in the inner circle during the Carter transition and part of the White House team. I had gained the confidence of Stuart Eizenstat, the president's top domestic policy advisor, and he asked me if I wanted to work for him and the president in the White House. But I knew Jim Schlesinger was to be energy secretary and figured correctly that Jim, not Stuart, would be the central focus of energy policy development. I therefore chose to be part of the Schlesinger-headed energy team that did indeed spend the first ninety days in office working closely with President Carter to hammer out his energy plan. President Carter made energy policy a high priority, never before or after duplicated by another president.

I was privileged to attend one major event during the transition at President-Elect Carter's home in Plains, Georgia. It was a meeting with the nation's environmental leaders at which the president-elect revealed that he had selected Cecil Andrus to be secretary of the interior. Before the meeting, I remember chatting with the president-elect's wife, Rosalynn Carter, who commented that she felt overwhelmed by gifts and all the details of moving to Washington. We forget that a new president's family faces serious relocation issues without a lot of help.

The highlight of the meeting was the environmental leaders' serious plea for the new president to name an environmental advisor with the same stature as the chief economic advisors, located right in the White House. Jimmy Carter listened patiently to what seemed a lengthy rationale supporting their request and said, "Yes, indeed—we will have an environmental advisor in the White House. It will be me! Folks, we won the election. I will be the environmentalist in the White House." And everyone had to laugh.

I was also witness to an important phone conversation during the transition between Jack Watson, a top advisor, and the president-elect. A senior congressional delegation had just met with Jack and urged that the president appoint someone experienced and trusted by Congress as the president's liaison to

Congress—and not Frank Moore, the aide from Georgia who was Carter's finance man. I heard Jack Watson repeat Jimmy Carter's reply: "Frank is my man, and he will be my man!" That's the moment the new president's relationship with Congress became a problem.

The time between Election Day, November 4, and January 20, when the new president is sworn in, is usually a waste of time. Despite all the advance thinking, the people who take office have their own ideas and are not inclined to adopt policy papers drafted before the election or during the transition. What really happens is a competitive free-for-all among the inner circle for promotions and influence. And it usually isn't very pretty. I was lucky, but a lot of good people got left out.

IN THE CARTER WHITE HOUSE

One of the most memorable days of my life was the second Sunday that President Carter was in office in January 1977. Jim Schlesinger, the future secretary of energy, was ill, and the president asked me to join him and Jody Powell, his press secretary, in his helicopter for an all-day trip from DC to Pittsburgh and back. A natural gas shortage was causing unemployment, and the president wanted to call attention to the problem. I received the invitation late on a Saturday and did well to make a few phone calls to industry executives to get some fragments of information about the situation.

Jody and I were seated quite close to President Carter on the helicopter as we took off and Jody Powell stated, "Mr. President, Jim is ill, but Dave is here with us, and he has a memo for you." President Carter saw my face turn pale because I had no memo. He didn't say a word—just picked up the newspaper and started reading. I nervously started writing what I knew on a pad of paper and then moved to the seat that faced him and briefed him, and he, in turn, jotted down a few notes. After a while, we were chatting away, and he made me feel so comfortable that I almost forgot I was shooting the breeze with the president of the United States. President Carter actually remembered facts from my Ford Foundation report titled "A Time to Choose" and walked back to where the press were seated and briefed them on the importance of energy efficiency.

Later in the day, I remarked that ammonium nitrate fertilizer plants consumed a large amount of natural gas. The president then suggested that we prepare and send to Congress legislation to authorize him to shut down the fertilizer plants and redirect the gas to industries that were closed because of the natural gas shortage in order to put people back to work. When he saw the worried look on my face, he said with a straight face, "Don't worry about the impact on the farmers. Remember that I am a farmer and I know how to handle them." I asked how, and he said, "You know the Spanish-speaking people we hired at the White House—we'll let them answer the phone calls." Yes, Jimmy Carter had a sense of humor and also felt if he did the right thing, everything would work out okay.

President Carter made the development of his energy policy the top priority in his first ninety days in office. It required an all-night work session, but we met the ninety-day deadline. I remember the president had the dozen of us who had prepared the policy with him in the rose garden as he announced it and said, "If you see those guys squinting, it's because they haven't seen the light of day for the last ninety days."

During the first six months of 1977, I had a large office in the old Executive Office Building as part of the president's energy team under Jim Schlesinger. In that role, I interacted with Congress, where I had worked as staff to the Senate Commerce Committee. One event through Congress resulted in a lifelong friendship. I traveled to Boston, Massachusetts, at the request of a then newly elected congressman named Ed Markey and appeared with him on a two-hour, primetime Boston radio program, all focused on energy policy. The now Senator Markey has never forgotten that event and has always listened to my views.

Jim Schlesinger was my boss, and I tried to help him in various ways. One was to arrange a meeting between him and Robert Redford. Jim and his wife had seven kids, so they never went to the movies, and Jim had no clue who Robert Redford was. But he found out when Redford arrived and every woman working in the White House was hanging out near Jim's office.

After the meeting, to which I wasn't invited, Redford stopped by my office in the Executive Office Building and said, "Jim Schlesinger is an actor." I asked what he meant by that, and he replied, "Jim said to me, 'There will never be a nuclear breeder reactor in your lifetime.' Dave, I am an actor, and I know a rehearsed line when I hear one. He was telling me what I wanted to hear, or he has a contract out on me."

In the first ninety days President Carter was in office, there was a sustained energy policy effort that focused on renewable energy efficiency and created the Department of Energy, where most of the White House energy team landed. But I had a different idea. My personal interest was in the Tennessee Valley Authority (TVA).

I asked Jim Schlesinger, who was the captain of our White House team, to inform the president of my desire. Jim and I were friends from the Nixon administration, but my views on energy policy had "turned green," and Jim's had not. A week or so later, I asked Jim what happened when he asked President Carter about my going to TVA, and at first, Jim didn't reply. When I pressed him, he said the president said, "Can you spare him?" At that moment, I knew Jim was going to back up my request.

The next step was a request from President Carter that I prepare a two- to three-page memo for him on the future of TVA. As Jim put it, this was a sort of take-home exam. The president already knew me, and he wanted to know what I proposed to do at TVA before he decided whether to appoint me to the job. The memo I prepared came back with a handwritten note on it from President Carter, asking that my ideas be put in a letter from the president to the current TVA chairman, Red Wagner. At first, I was unhappy that the president was stealing my ideas, until I realized I had not only passed the exam, but the president wanted to adopt these ideas as his own.

President Carter announced his decision to nominate me for the TVA board vacancy on July 15, 1977, and the Senate promptly began its hearings on the nomination on August 1. The Senate committee hearings under Chairman Randolph of West Virginia appeared to be going smoothly, but there was trouble on the horizon. Senator Sasser, newly elected from Tennessee, refused to endorse me and asked a bunch of troublesome questions at my nomination hearing. Senator Hollings—who, out of friendship, sat next to me at my confirmation hearing—vividly pointed out that one senator from Tennessee could kill my nomination all by himself. At Senator Hollings's urgent command, I went up to Senator Sasser's office as soon as hearings recessed.

As I walked into his private office, the senator looked at me and said, "I hate you—nothing personal, but I'm going to keep hating you for quite some time. I knocked myself out traveling over the hills of Tennessee campaigning for your president, yet he doesn't even have the courtesy to ask for my advice in filling the most important federal position in the state. We may agree on everything, but you are gonna be in trouble with me for a long time." Senator Sasser did not hold up my nomination, but he was as good as his word in giving me a hard time for quite a while. He held hearings, even questioning TVA's expenditures for air pollution control needed to comply with the federal Air Quality Law.

I also managed to get into trouble with the senator Howard Baker, who was my friend, when I testified at my confirmation hearing by expressing my negative views on his favorite project: the nuclear breeder reactor being built at Oak Ridge, Tennessee. I finally agreed that as TVA director, I would not try to kill the project. Senator Baker, a Republican, could have easily killed my nomination, but he was graciously forgiving and, in fact, supportive despite my unforgivable candor.

A more serious opposition to my nomination came from Senator Stennis, who then was probably the most powerful senator, chairing both the defense and appropriations committees in the Senate. Jim Schlesinger was of great help when he came along with me when I met privately with the senator. Jim was a former defense secretary, and the senator admired him. After an hour of friendly chatter with Senator Stennis, Jim left. Senator Stennis then said, "I've never seen Big Jim sit that long for anyone; the president must be pretty serious about you."

"Yes, sir," I mumbled, and the senator asked me whether it was true I was a radical environmentalist. I said, "No, sir, I am a practical environmentalist."

The senator then said, "Practical environmentalist—I think we can live with that, but there is another problem. Martin McClain, the publisher of the Tupelo, Mississippi, newspaper, is worried that you are a no-growth guy, and his newspaper is pitched out to every porch in town, so it wouldn't be good for either you or me if he were against you." I readily agreed to meet with Mr. McClain, the publisher, who turned out to be a New Deal Democrat who at once not only endorsed me but became an admirer. He actually hosted a large welcoming lunch for me in Tupelo after I became director.

Despite these hiccups, I was promptly confirmed and sworn in at the White House in late August 1977. I felt empowered to redirect TVA to become an example of clean air and renewable energy that made efficiency a big deal. I departed DC and reached Tennessee just before Labor Day.

Reforming The TVA

Going back to Knoxville was a major fork in the road not only in my career but in my then twenty-seven-year marriage. Marianne really didn't want to go back to Knoxville, so we split for the time being without a clear understanding of our future as a couple. Our three kids were all in or starting college, so our family was really splitt—and, as it turned out, split for good.

I vividly remember the excitement and, indeed, exuberance I felt as I drove my little Opel Kadett down to Tennessee. In fact, I was so excited that I picked up a speeding ticket in Virginia along the way. I spent Labor Day Weekend camping in the Smoky Mountains near Knoxville and feeling a sense of freedom and challenge that can best be described as a *giant ego trip*. Here was a guy who did well to even get a job with TVA when he graduated from Georgia Tech coming back as the top dog and living as a free man for the first time in decades.

Very few people have had the fortune of the giant ego trip I enjoyed as the head of TVA. One day, I had an afternoon meeting with Governor Hunt of North Carolina at Fontana Dam in that state and an evening speaking engagement at Georgia Tech in Atlanta. I had to fly in the TVA helicopter to get to my speech on time. Imagine my feeling of pride and power as I flew over Peachtree Street in Atlanta at a low altitude and landed at the Georgia Tech practice field.

I did not just feel this excitement and joy at my job; they also permeated my personal life. I felt like a kid who had just been set free. I recall how happy I was just to play tennis with a neighbor, Jean Solari, without even seeing her after the tennis match. I had been in a nuclear family for twenty-seven years, and being able to interact with people—men and women—as I wished gave me a new form of freedom that made me very happy. It also told me more than I wanted to know about the state of my marriage because I had no desire to share all this with my wife.

At first, I was just a member of the three-person TVA board. The other two members—the chairman, Red Wagner, and Bill Jenkins, whose policies were essentially the opposite of mine—were in clear control. Chairman Wagner's term ended more than six months later, in May 1978. I knew the first months would mainly be a listening and learning experience for me. But unwisely, I did a lot more than listen.

During the first week on the job, I stopped by the local newspaper's office for what I considered a courtesy call, but I was so full of myself that I got into substance. I called the Tellico Dam and the small snail darter fish it threatened a "relatively minor issue." (It was a big deal.) Even worse, I referred to Secretary of Energy Schlesinger's remark that the nuclear breeder reactor located in Oak Ridge was a technological turkey. I came close to breaking my promise to Senator Baker. The best I can say is that I was determined to tell what I considered the truth. A retrospective assessment shows that I was inexperienced and politically naïve.

Another initial meeting worth recording was with Lee "Tat" Anderson, a high school buddy who was the editor of the *Chattanooga Times Free Press*, one of the most conservative newspapers in America at the time. I asked Tat if I was going to have to read about TVA being Socialist in his paper. He said, "No, Dave, of course TVA is still Socialist, but after fifty years, you're our Socialist, and we love you." And indeed, his paper was by and large supportive of TVA, including a new TVA office building that caused many local landlords to lose their TVA tenants.

I made quite an effort to recruit new blood to help me transform TVA into a green yardstick. I was successful in hiring people from as far as Massachusetts, Colorado, and Texas. One of those folks, Bob King from Austin, Texas, told me that what attracted him to TVA was a speech I gave in Atlanta. According to

Bob, I said I wanted to hire folks who would be innovative enough so that some things they tried actually failed. A boss so dedicated to innovation that he would accept failure convinced Bob King I was really serious about reforming TVA.

TVA's nuclear power program—while wildly popular—had created a small but very active group of antinuclear activists who regularly attended TVA board meetings and voiced their angry disapproval. They viewed me as a friend. I thought I could help calm them down before I had a majority of the board with me, so I agreed to have lunch with them at the end of my first TVA board meeting. When I told Chairman Wagner what I was doing, he only half-jokingly said he would send over the TVA security guard to protect me.

At lunch, one of the activists, who lived near the construction site of the Huntsville 4 unit nuclear plant, claimed TVA was deliberately harassing her by blowing a loud horn every morning at 4:00 a.m. I told her that the horn simply signaled a new shift of working people and quickly got the construction manager to stop it. These critics and TVA were clearly not on speaking terms. The irony of that meeting is that five years later, my vote stopped construction of that plant altogether.

During those first six months, I mostly listened at public board meetings, but between meetings, I raised lots of questions to TVA staff. They started calling my questions *Dave-o-grams*. Lynn Seeber, a general manager who was a personal friend from my days as a TVA staff member, offered to buy me a television set so I would watch TV and spend less time writing questions for staff.

My questioning of staff reached a climax after three months on the job, when Chairman Wagner and General Manager Seeber invited me into the chairman's office and accused me of severely hurting morale because staff really couldn't answer my questions. I replied that we indeed had a problem, and one solution was getting more knowledgeable staff. That ended the conversation and the attempt to shut me up.

The first issue I actually raised at a private board agenda meeting was about automobiles. The board needed to approve the purchase of a large number of new cars, and the staff proposed full-size sedans. I suggested that we could save money and energy by buying smaller, more fuel-efficient cars, not really expecting any support. But to my delight, Director Jenkins said maybe I had a point and suggested we defer action till the next board meeting. As we adjourned, the six-foot-two-inch general manager Lynn Seeber and his equally tall finance chief asked me to come down to the TVA garage with them. Lynn demonstrated how difficult it was for them to get into one of the small cars. I then said, "We do have a problem, gentlemen—we either need larger cars or smaller managers." They didn't laugh, and a few months later, my personal friend Mr. Seeber resigned.

Shortly after I arrived on the TVA scene, I got some very good advice from the longtime mayor of Oak Ridge. He said, "TVA is big and powerful and runs roughshod over us little folks. Leave us a few crumbs, and we will be okay." It was advice that I remembered but didn't really follow until years later, after having tried to run roughshod over my opponents most of my life. The one person who put me in my place during my early pre-chairman months as a TVA director was Mary Aubry, my executive secretary. She gave me a T-shirt at Christmas with Our Savior in big letters, a sarcastic kick in the pants that I needed but didn't heed.

The two big issues I faced in the early months before I became chairman were the Tellico Dam on the Little Tennessee River in East Tennessee and compliance with the federal Clean Air Act. The Tellico Dam was already built before I became a board member, but environmental activists had obtained a federal court order stopping TVA from closing the gates to create the lake behind the dam. The court ruled that the dam, if completed, would endanger a small fish protected by the federal Endangered Species Act called the snail darter. The issue of the dam versus the tiny fish made national news, and the controversy brought into question the very existence of the Endangered Species Act. The idea that preserving a tiny fish species was not worth closing an already-built dam fueled a major effort to repeal the basic law that protected all endangered species.

TVA had already taken the position that it was exempt from the Endangered Species Act, and the case was pending before the Supreme Court. I disagreed politically with the TVA position and felt we needed to abide by the law and not create a lake that would kill the fish. I quickly became known as "Dry Dam" Freeman on thousands of bumper stickers all over East Tennessee. I was, of course, in the minority at the time and could not even get my point of view stated in the legal brief before the Supreme Court.

The TVA lawyers bitterly resented my taking a public position opposite their opinion that TVA was exempt from the Endangered Species Act. Senior TVA lawyers threatened to resign. I went downstairs to their offices and reminded them that it was their job to give me legal advice, but if I thought they were wrong, the position I took on an issue was my decision, not theirs. They calmed down but were still resentful.

The Supreme Court's 9–0 decision encouraged me that TVA was wrong and I was correct in that TVA was indeed subject to the Endangered Species Act and had to protect the snail darter. TVA was thus forbidden to close the dam's gates. But local pressure to complete the dam was intense, and the controversy just got hotter. I proposed selling the land that TVA had set aside for the lake back to the original landowners, but that was not legally possible.

I then held a public hearing on the subject, which attracted hundreds of people in favor of closing the dam gates. I can recall one lady's testimony as if it was yesterday. She got up and said, "When TVA took my daddy's farm and promised us a lake, I didn't cry, but if TVA doesn't give us that lake, I will cry." Local Congresspeople were under intense pressure to change the law.

The final word came when Congress passed a bill in the dead of night that directed TVA to close the gate and complete the Tellico Project, "notwithstanding any other provision of law." We did just that. The Endangered Species Act as a whole survived, and so did the snail darter, which TVA transplanted to the Hiwassee River, where it lived happily ever after. I did not lose my sense of humor over that setback. I phoned my friend Senator Baker, who had sponsored the complete-the-dam legislation, and joked that I was bringing in some Mexicans to close the gate and save money since his law said to finish the dam, "notwithstanding any other provision of law." We had a good laugh, and the senator said, "Just close the gates and end the fuss."

When I joined the TVA board, the agency was in flagrant violation of the federal Air Quality Act; indeed, it was the worst polluter of sulfur dioxide (SO_2) in the nation. We faced a lawsuit filed by the EPA and supported by local agencies, such as the State of Alabama. I persuaded my fellow board members, with the support of the TVA staff, to authorize me to negotiate a settlement with the EPA, since I knew the EPA chief. I kept the other board members informed as I made progress, and they gave me the impression they were in agreement with the terms being considered.

The final agreement was a big deal; we would cut our SO_2 emissions in half by investing about a billion dollars in pollution control equipment to pay for the cleanup. Electric rates that were about four cents per kilowatt-hour would have to go up 7 percent, about one-fourth of a cent. I felt confident that the other two board members would approve the settlement, since the TVA staff had endorsed the negotiations and supported the settlement because they feared a worse result from the lawsuit.

The settlement included a novel provision under which the folks who sued TVA would constitute a group to follow progress in the implementation with authority to report on progress, or lack thereof, to the federal court that approved the settlement. That provision proved to be quite a stumbling block.

When I presented the final settlement agreement, the existing board members' reaction was shocking. Bill Jenkins actually resigned from the board, stating that he didn't believe in the air quality law that would cause TVA to increase rates by 7 percent. That left TVA, in the spring of 1978, with just two board members: me and Chairman Wagner. I was pleased when Chairman Wagner assured me he would approve the settlement if it eliminated the provision allowing the parties who sued us to monitor progress. That was a week before his term expired.

I worked the phones all one weekend and got approval to delete the provision to placate Chairman Wagner. But with only a few days left in his term, Chairman Wagner still refused to approve the settlement and didn't offer any explanation. So the settlement was on hold for six months till another board member took office.

Unlike Chairman Wagner, who chose to just fade away, I admired Director Jenkins, despite fundamentally disagreeing with him, for resigning when he felt he couldn't agree with what we needed to do to obey the law. Bill was a genuine reflection of East Tennessee's belief in limited government. He also had a great sense of humor, once advising me that as a new board member who was going to take control, if I "fed those turkeys all year long, I wouldn't cut their throat at Thanksgiving." In other words, get rid of the deadwood before they become friends.

Chairman Wagner retired on May 18, 1978, and President Carter then named me TVA board chairman as of that date. A week earlier, I met with President Carter in the Oval Office. He greeted me warmly but remarked that I seemed to be chasing the other directors away. Director Jenkins had resigned, and Chairman Wagner was retiring in a week, and I would then be alone. I replied that I was just trying to make him the first president since Roosevelt to appoint all three member of the TVA board. The president then suggested I try to implement our reforms with a lot less fanfare—in other words, cool off. He then asked if I knew any businessman he could appoint whom I could work with.

I said, "Yes, sir, his name is Richard Freeman."

The president then said, "Dave, I can't appoint your brother to the TVA board."

I said, "Sir, he is not my brother; he is the head of a railroad."

When the president interviewed Richard Freeman, the first question he asked was, "Are you any kin to Dave?" Richard Freeman and I served seven years together and agreed on every issue. We remained good friends for more than fifty years, from the time he was a TVA lawyer who influenced me, the unhappy engineer, to go to law school in 1954, until he passed away.

President Carter accepted my invitation to come to the Tennessee Valley and give a major speech about TVA that I drafted just as Chairman Wagner retired and I became chairman and the only board member. The event made clear that I had the president's personal support. He then appointed Richard Freeman as a director, and by September 1978, when Richard was confirmed, we finally had a quorum (two votes out of three) to take action as the Freeman Board.

Dick, who passed away at age ninety, and I had what turned out to be a final dinner in DC in July 2011. He joked that I had ruined his reputation before he got there. He then got serious and recalled that we reached agreement on every major issue over a seven-year period. We had such respect for each other's opinions that, according to Dick, we often ended up advocating the opposing view than we had to begin with.

From May to September 1978, I was the only TVA board member and had the awkward role of being the "boss" but without a quorum. Under the law, I could not initiate any new actions. I could only take actions necessary to pursue existing policies. I was much too aggressive about asserting my role as chairman and earned a reputation for being arrogant. Arrogance was sort of inherent to being the single person bossing fifty thousand TVA employees. And as President Carter had foreseen, it didn't help that the nominee in waiting was also named Freeman. (Cartoons about cloning were abundant.) But I removed any doubt about my arrogance at the first public board meeting where I presided alone.

The staff had arranged for two top staff people to sit on each side of me in the seats of the two other nonexistent board members. I visibly directed them to leave these seats and return to their staff seats. As a result, the front page of the local paper reported on my arrogant behavior. I did keep the lights on and rates stable, so there was no revolt.

A clear signal of the TVA employees' opinion of me occurred when I fell and busted my back when I was the lonely chairman. A TVA employee was quoted (not by name) in the press saying, "I hope he broke it." I did heal completely, but only by sleeping on the floor for a couple of weeks. That accident didn't shut me up or even slow me down.

After Dick Freeman was confirmed, the first action of the Freeman Board was to approve the air quality settlement that I previously negotiated. TVA's distributors met this action with strong disapproval, and many local officials opposed anything that raised the price of electricity, even if it was for cleaner air. The TVA distributors actually sued TVA, trying to stop the clean air investments. And Senator Sasser, true to his word, held hearings questioning our investments in pollution control. We beat back these efforts and went ahead, completing the cleanup on time and within our budget. And in so doing, TVA cut its sulfur dioxide emissions in half!

TVA played an important role in Congress's passage of acid-rain legislation in 1979, which successfully reduced pollution from coal-fired power plants. Pollution from power plants was producing acid rain, which polluted water in lakes many hundreds of miles from the plants. Previously, tall stacks that dispersed the pollution over areas of hundreds of miles were the norm. Dilution, it turned out, was not a solution to pollution.

TVA was the only utility that supported the acid-rain legislation, and we provided Congress with hard facts about the relatively low cost of any cleanup effort. We were of crucial help to Congress. I testified in favor of the legislation, much to the lasting anger of coal-state senators from the valley. That sort of set the pattern for my TVA board years, 1977–1984.

We launched major additional initiatives for energy efficiency, for the use of solar energy, for stopping the construction of eight large nuclear plants that cost too much, for pioneering the use of electric cars, and on and on. These were the programs I promised President Carter we would initiate and pursue. And Dick and I kept our promise. We were not popular in the Tennessee Valley, which was in love with nuclear power, in part because Oak Ridge, Tennessee, was the home of the atomic bomb.

While we were making TVA much more environmentally sensitive, we also took actions needed to ensure that TVA was able to meet its basic responsibility as the source of reliable, low-cost power. An early issue was the TVA Act's limit on the amount of money TVA could borrow. Even with a program that focused on efficiency, we needed to borrow more than the TVA Act allowed. Amending the TVA Act was a risky proposition, as it gave private power companies an opportunity to offer amendments that could cripple us.

We succeeded in getting the limit raised from $26 billion to $35 billion, without any crippling amendments, by promising to confine TVA retail sales to within our existing service area. We had serious opposition from the private power companies, who preferred that TVA wither and fade away. We got some help with Congress from friends like Charlie Curtis, deputy secretary of energy, but what was crucial was TVA had powerful friends from the valley in Congress who supported TVA without question.

Living as a Local Big Shot

After I became TVA chairman in 1978, I became a very public figure in Knoxville, Tennessee, the buckle of the Bible Belt. My personal life was complicated. My marriage to Marianne was over by the time I became chairman, but we were still legally married. She was living in DC, and I was in Knoxville. Agreeing on the terms of a divorce dragged on, even though the kids were all in college and we didn't have much money to divide. It took until 1980 before we reached an agreement.

In the meantime, my social life as a single man stayed quite private but was nonetheless enjoyable and a learning experience for me. In my fifty-one years, I had never before had any women friends. When I was a kid, girls were only girlfriends, not some of the guys. And during my twenty-eight years of marriage, we were a nuclear family, and my social life happened as a couple interacting with other couples, except for the few other male friends I had.

One of the first female friends I made was Jean Solari, a TVA employee who lived in a condo just a few doors away from me. I remember the simple joy of sharing thoughts about people with her. When I fell and busted my back, I had to sleep on the floor. She brought me work from the office and cooked a meal, but there was never, ever any romance. Instead, we shared personal stuff and have remained lifelong friends.

Friendships with women opened a new dimension to my social life because, unlike most men, women speak about their feelings and listen to your personal joys and frustrations. To be sure, I was not immune to romance, but I was mindful of the fact that I was the CEO of an outfit that employed much more than fifteen thousand women.

I fell head over heels in love with one woman, and she loved me. But it was not meant to be, for she worked at TVA. If I have ever done anything unselfish in my life, it was letting go of her before it ruined her promising career—as it would have in those days. I even considered asking President Carter to give me another job if he got reelected, but he didn't. I know in my heart I did the right thing.

Because Knoxville is near the buckle of the Bible Belt, my dating activities faced considerable public scrutiny. When one dear friend went to Africa with me when I attended a conference on large dams, I didn't reveal that she went along even though we were both single. It was a great trip.

I did exercise considerable self-control with respect to my executive secretary, Mary Aubry, who was both bright and beautiful. It was only years later that she told me she had a crush on me at that time. She said I revealed my feelings only once, when I yelled at her, "Don't we have a dress code around here?" on a Saturday when she was wearing tight-fitting blue jeans. She left TVA to finish her education and became a successful attorney. She and I continue to be close friends.

I stayed in touch with my three kids while living in Knoxville and running TVA, but they may have a different view on whether I seemed distant or close. I do remember visiting my daughter, Anita, at Ann Arbor while she went to the University of Wisconsin. The taste of the great ice cream we had lingers on. I also managed to persuade her to go to the Caribbean island of Saint John with me for a few days, and she did visit me at least once in Knoxville. As to my sons, Stan and Roger, I had similar experiences at their colleges, Cornell and the University of Michigan.

I also managed to persuade each of my three kids to go on a foreign trip with me. Anita and Stan each went on separate trips, to China and Israel. Roger went to Israel with me and my mom in 1973. My kids and I have remained close friends. I have not tried to tell them what to do, and I am immensely proud of what they accomplished on their own. I financed their college tuition but not their beer. It's worked out fine.

I made probably the best move of my life in 2011, from my condo near the beach in Marina del Rey, California, to downtown DC. I moved to be near Anita and Stan and their seven total children—my grandchildren. And now there is Charlie, the great-grandchild who arrived in August 2014. For the first time since 1976, I actually live in the same town as my family. For thirty-nine years, I had no family, not even a cousin, in the town where I lived. I am so lucky that I wised up in time to get acquainted with the day-to-day life of my family. It's a real joy.

As TVA chairman, I met a lot of people, but the most interesting was Bill Clinton. He was the young governor of Arkansas back in 1978, when he invited me to talk to him about obtaining TVA power for West Memphis, Arkansas, just across the Mississippi River from Memphis, Tennessee. He claimed West Memphis was hurting economically because of TVA's lower electric rates in Memphis and asked if TVA could serve West Memphis.

What I recall most clearly about my first meeting with Bill Clinton is that he knew more details about the history of TVA than I did. He said he'd done a paper on TVA in college. Unfortunately, our effort to enable TVA to serve West Memphis was blocked by Congress, which had enacted a wall around the TVA service area. The private power companies killed our attempt to punch a little hole in the wall for West Memphis.

So, back in 1978, I learned what the whole world has since learned—Bill Clinton is as smart and as much fun to be around as anyone on earth. My memory is that Governor Clinton was extremely progressive and fearless in his first term. Once, at a Southern governor meeting at the Rockefeller estate in Arkansas, I made a speech blasting the oil industry. Bill Clinton stood up next and gave the shortest speech of his life: "I agree with Dave." I fell in love with the guy on the spot and treasure every moment I've been in his presence. I am one of the thousands of folks who feel as if Bill Clinton is their friend. We feel that way because he is. It is in that context that I relate one of the more interesting conversations I had with him.

In 1979, right after he was defeated in a reelection bid, Bill Clinton was a guest speaker in TVA territory in West Kentucky. I was not in attendance, but at about midnight that night, I received a phone call from a female TVA employee who did attend. She said she wanted to get some advice for how to respond to the ex-governor of Arkansas suggesting she go to bed with him. I said the way to respond was to put the SOB on the phone so I could make sure he was there and they were joking around with me.

He said, "Dave, why aren't you here? You invited me and didn't even show."

I said, "Bill, that's my woman. Leave her alone."

He again replied, "Why aren't you here?"

I saw my employee in the normal course of business a few weeks later and asked what happened. She smiled and said, "You'll never know." Of course, if they weren't having fun playing a joke on me, they would never have called me. It was Bill's way of getting my attention, just like an ordinary buddy would do.

Al Gore was just a member of the House of Representatives when I was chairman of the TVA board. Unlike other younger members of the valley delegation in Congress, he supported TVA even when we raised the rates. We became friends, and he often called to ask for favors. One day, back in 1978, when I was bored, I answered my own phone when he called. He asked, "Do you always answer your own phone?"

I answered, "Only when an important person calls." There was a fifteen-second pause while his IQ of 170 tried to figure out how I knew before he laughed at my joke.

Another famous person I had the privilege of meeting was David Lilienthal, who was a founding member of the TVA board in 1933 and later became the chairman of the AEC. We traveled through the Tennessee Valley together, and he told me of two episodes worth recalling. One was a meeting early in TVA's history in one of the valley cities—I believe Guntersville, Alabama. At a large town meeting, the mayor asked Director Lilienthal, "What will TVA do for Guntersville?"

Lilienthal answered, "Absolutely nothing," paused, and then said, "until Guntersville decides what it wants to do for itself. And then we will help." That was the TVA philosophy throughout the years.

The other event involved how the TVA promotional rates were developed. That rate schedule provided lower rates for greater use and thus encouraged the widespread use of electricity. It was the opposite of today's focus on higher rates for more use to encourage the more efficient use of electricity.

I asked Mr. Lilienthal if the original TVA rates were based on costs. And he said, "Oh my gosh, no! Our first source of power was from the Wilson Dam at Muscle Shoals, Alabama, and the costs certainly didn't go down with volume. We were simply trying to promote the greater use of electricity and encourage people to live better electrically." He said they didn't make any studies; "just a few guys in a cabin in the woods one weekend decided on it."

A couple of episodes at TVA live in my head as lessons learned about large organizations. One observation is that the more people are in the chain of command, the more likely mistakes are to occur. The other is that in a large outfit, people will do almost anything rather than disobey their immediate boss.

One day while working at TVA headquarters in Knoxville, I had an important dinner meeting with civic leaders in Russellville, Kentucky. I asked my secretary to arrange for the TVA airplane to take me there. She in turn had to call the travel coordinator, who in turn had to call the pilot. Somewhere along the chain of calls, *Russellville, Kentucky,* became just *Russellville,* and I ended up in Russellville, Alabama, a city familiar to our flight people because it was near large TVA facilities. I discovered the mistake only when I landed and no one greeted me, except a sign saying RUSSELLVILLE, ALABAMA. I made a phone call to my dinner hosts in Kentucky, got back on my plane, and finally reached my destination to find folks had gotten pretty drunk waiting for me. I got quite a rousing response to a very short speech.

The other episode came on a day when I took one phone call too many before leaving for the airport to catch a commercial flight that wouldn't wait for me. At TVA, we had a fifty-year custom of board members driving themselves—no chauffeurs. By the time I got to the TVA garage where my TVA car was parked, I knew I'd miss the plane if I had to find a parking spot at the airport. I therefore politely asked the female staff person in the garage if she'd drive me to the airport. She politely but firmly said no. I asked her if she knew who I was. She said, "Sure, Chairman Freeman, I know who you are, but I'm not authorized to drive TVA cars by the rules down here. I know you are the top man, but my immediate boss enforces the rules. I'd get in real trouble if I drove you." Her real boss then showed up and took me to the airport.

I learned a great lesson about consumers' attitudes toward electric rates from the greatest teacher of all—personal experience. The basic lesson was that, to the average customer, the utility was a company they loved to hate. After all, they have nothing else in their lives that is an absolute necessity that they never see and they don't know how much they buy, and they get blacked out if they don't pay the utility bill on time. So, if you raise the rates, ordinary customers just want to vent their anger so you hear the hardships you are imposing on them. The last thing they wish to hear is an explanation that justifies the rate increase. That is why elected city council folks cannot do a fair job of deciding the rate increase required by city-owned electric power utilities.

I learned this lesson in Rogersville, Tennessee, at a hearing conducted by the congressman Jimmy Quillen, who represented the area for many years. The hearing was to discuss a sizable TVA rate increase. I presented a chart that showed even with the electric rate increase, the rate in the Rogersville area was much lower than the electric rates in Atlanta, Georgia, and Birmingham, Alabama. Mr. Quillen stated rather bluntly, "Mr. Freeman, that chart is out of order. If my people wanted to live in Atlanta or Birmingham, they would move there. They live in Rogersville—you are raising the rates in Rogersville. That's what this hearing is all about."

ENERGY EFFICIENCY

Of all the initiatives by the Freeman Board, the energy efficiency program was unique, being both popular with retail customers and wildly successful. We reached about five hundred thousand customers and conserved the equivalent of a large nuclear power plant at a small fraction of the cost. The program worked because we made it easy for the customer to participate. TVA hired *energy doctors* who made house calls. The doctors prescribed cost-effective efficiency measures in homes and businesses, including electric heat pumps, and the customer would choose a contractor on the spot from an approved list. TVA would inspect the work and pay the contractor. The customer would repay the loan as part of his or her utility bill, which would still get reduced by the energy saved during the payback period of five years or less. After the payback period, their bill would reduce much more. The loans were 99 percent repaid. People paid their utility bills.

The nation's utilities would do well to adopt such a program today; it was a success because people didn't have to invest their money or do anything but sign their name. The energy efficiency program reduced people's electric bills and was popular with the public, but not with most of the managers of the 150 cities and co-ops that distributed TVA power at retail. Under the TVA Act, we controlled their rates. They were already bitterly opposed to our actions to abide by the Clean Air Act, which caused rates to rise. They were interested in selling more power, rather than the efficiency program we installed.

To understand the distributor's point of view, it is useful to recall that TVA was the Walmart of the utility industry; TVA's legally mandated mission is to sell electricity at the lowest possible price. Before the Freemans arrived, TVA resisted every environmental law more forcefully than even a privately owned utility. *Low price* was a religion to TVA, so it resisted spending money to control pollution, reclaim the strip-mined land that supplied coal for TVA plants, or clean the air.

To be sure, everyone older than forty, including members of Congress, had an unshakable loyalty to TVA. So I got the benefit of that "mother love." But my emphasis on environmental protection and my antinuclear activism tried their patience. As my confirmation experience with Senator Stennis revealed, I was saved by the strength of their gratitude for what TVA accomplished in bringing that seven-state area out of poverty and into the middle class. I was quite aware that the TVA distributors felt unhappy, and therefore, I embarked on a series of one-on-one meetings with all the 150 managers. In retrospect, those meetings were a mistake because they resulted in frank exchanges of views on environmental issues that just hardened the opposition to me personally.

One of the highlights of my TVA years was in 1980, President Carter invited me to attend his famous summit meeting at Camp David, where he reviewed his basic approach to a variety of issues. Energy was one of the most prominent ones. The president had no problem with TVA, and it was not discussed. There was a major discussion about whether the government should take action to restrict oil imports. The energy secretary, Jim Schlesinger, and I debated the issue in the president's presence. I urged action to reduce imports, and Jim was opposed to such restrictions on free trade. The president, in his post-summit *malaise* speech—which never used that word—announced a policy of reducing oil imports but, importantly, did not specify a tariff or any other specific action to implement his policy.

Secretary Schlesinger resigned shortly after the Camp David summit and was replaced byMr. Duncan, a Coca-Cola executive.

Shortly after taking office, Secretary Duncan asked me to go to Washington, DC, to meet with him. At the meeting, he said, "Dave, you talked the president into promising to reduce oil imports. Well, it's not an option in the Energy Department briefing book. Please tell me, how can we do it?" I said that one way was a tariff on imported oil. He then kept taking phone calls as I tried to suggest other options. It was clear to me he was going through a drill and had little interest in really implementing President Carter's policy. At any rate, President Carter's term was about over, and President Reagan had a totally different view. His policies were, in summary, the opposite of President Carter's.

My TVA tenure included a trip to China and Pakistan in 1980. Vice President Mondale asked me to head a delegation of engineers in China, which included the chief of the Corps of Engineers and others. Our mission was to help the Chinese develop their hydropower and to create a friendly tie to the Chinese government, which President Carter had only recently recognized.

We landed in Beijing, then a city with *no* automobiles, just a sea of bicycles, but with terrible air pollution from burning charcoal for heating homes and coal for power production. The only cars I saw were a few Russian limousines, which were very long. And as head of the delegation, I rode in one and stayed in guesthouses with bathrooms the size of American apartments. We drove down the middle of the street; the only other traffic was bicycles.

Our team traveled throughout eastern China, giving advice to Chinese engineers planning to harness China's vast hydroelectric potential. We saw rural China, where people worked relentlessly, carrying water and working on the farms seven days a week. Many of the people we encountered had never seen a white person. They were curious and friendly. In fact, the Chinese kids in some villages followed me like pied pipers marching down the street with me. I got them all to sing, "USA, USA!"

We saw rural China in the raw. Once, I took a picture with my Polaroid camera of a young lady walking past our car stuck in the mud. She thought I was some kind of God when I handed her the picture of herself. She handed me the handmade hat she was wearing, and I was told I must accept it. Then I heard a voice shouting from a nearby house. It was her father saying, "Get away from those white devils."

A highlight of the trip was a public meeting concerning whether the Chinese should build the Three Gorges Dam. Our delegation advised the Chinese to postpone construction and build smaller dams they could complete in a year or two, rather than tying up all the construction equipment in China for a decade at Three Gorges. It was unusual that the head of the Chinese water and power administration disagreed with the Chinese electric power agency in public—just a little bit of transparency in the Chinese government.

Our delegation proved helpful to the Chinese national government in convincing local officials of the value of the proposed hydro projects. The local officials had serious political problems with building the dams because it would displace their people. Much to my surprise, I learned that the national government needed the local government's consent because projects don't get built without local approval. Politics—public opinion—does play a role in China. An example is one dam site we visited just downstream of the Three Gorges site. Construction was underway, but I asked why. It seemed out of sequence. The Chinese construction manager said, "Premier Chou came by here last year and promised these people a dam." Politics are local everywhere.

The China trip ended with a meeting between me and a Chinese vice premier in the Great Hall of the People in Beijing. We signed an agreement to exchange visits of Chinese and American engineers and useful information. We achieved our objective. I still recall that the Chinese vice premier became angry and felt insulted when I suggested China could borrow the money to build their dams in response to his plea of poverty. At the time, they thought only poor people borrowed money and I had insulted him. The Chinese view of economics has really changed since then.

The TVA delegation went from China to Pakistan. There, I signed an agreement to exchange experts and information with Pakistan's Water and Power Administration. The head of the Water and Power Administration was General Butt, who had built the highway from Pakistan to China at twenty thousand feet. He told me that the Water and Power Administration was patterned after TVA and I was the first TVA person ever to visit them. He took us up to see the Tarbela Dam on the Afghan border, the largest earth-filled dam in the world. When we reached an agreement, General Butt said, "Praise Allah," so I just said, "Praise Allah." It was a successful trip.

The year 1980 was the foreign-travel year for me at TVA. I also accepted an invitation to attend the dedication of a solar pond in Israel and learn more about Israel's solar programs. The idea was to form a shallow pond in the hot Israeli sun and extract heat to run a turbine. The solar pond idea died when the price of oil plunged in the 1980s. But one event left a lasting impression.

The automobile ride from Jerusalem to the solar panel dedication near the Dead Sea was quite an adventure. The chief scientist of Israel took me and Hugh Parris, TVA's manager of power, into his personal care. We ran out of gas in Hebron, a Palestinian city. His understatement was "This is not a good place to run out of gas," and then he walked off to find gas. We sat very still in the car for about an hour until he returned unharmed with a can of gas. When we arrived at the dedication, we discovered that a group came on a bus and Arab people had stoned it as they drove through Hebron. We were lucky.

During that visit to Israel, I met with the chairman of Israel Electric, who happened to be a retired general in the Israel Defense Forces. At the time, the Iranians were holding a group of American citizens hostage. At lunch for just the two of us, I asked him what he would do if he were in President Carter's shoes. At first, he said, "It's too late; the Middle East is a jungle. You must have plans in advance." I persisted, and after a few very short pauses, he said,

"I'd drop a whole bunch of parachute troops on Tehran to distract the Iranians—but they would be dummies. In the meantime, we land paratroops. I'd kidnap the Ayatollah; we know where he lives. Then I'd negotiate the release of the hostages."

I did relay this conversation to a friend in the Department of Defense, but I'm sure President Carter never heard it. The Israeli general's point was that you need to live in the jungle to know how to survive.

THE REAGAN YEARS

In January 1981, Ronald Reagan was sworn in as president. As a result, I was demoted from TVA board chairman, but my term of office as a director did not expire until May 1984. Republican Senator Baker of Tennessee asked me to stay on, and Richard Freeman, as director, and I still constituted a majority of the three-person board. TVA was an independent agency, and Dick and I continued the focus on efficiency, solar energy, and innovation that was in the best interest of TVA ratepayers and the environment. We were also determined to deal with the runaway cost and safety concerns of constructing nuclear power plants. And we had the protection of the mother love of powerful members of Congress from the Tennessee Valley—both Republicans and Democrats.

Strangely enough, Ronald Reagan's defeat of Jimmy Carter in 1980 did not diminish my authority at TVA. To be sure, Charles Dean replaced me as chairman of the board, but Dick Freeman and I still controlled board decisions as joint CEO. In fact, our most important accomplishments on nuclear power took place in the 1981–1984 period, when Reagan was president. And we continued our solar power and energy efficiency efforts without any change.

My mother actually paid more attention to the new president than I did. One day, I asked for her opinion of President Reagan, and she said, "Some good, some bad." She then explained the good was that he supported Israel. "The bad, son—he cheated you out of three thousand dollars." I politely told her she was confused, and she replied, "It is a shame that my own son can't remember what he told his own mother—that when Reagan became president, he named someone else as TVA chairman and reduced your salary by three thousand dollars." Her answer is classic grassroots politics; she judged the president by the two most important things in her life—Israel and her family.

My mother had happily lived in my dad's shadow during their forty-five years of married life, but after he passed away, I became increasingly aware of what a strong yet modest person my mother was. She was truly grateful for any good that came her way, and while strong, she was never demanding or even felt entitled to more than she had. But I digress.

The dominant challenge of my TVA board experience was over nuclear power. When I joined the board in 1977, TVA had ten large, one-thousand-megawatt nuclear power plants under construction. They projected growth in electricity consumption that was unreal to me and in direct conflict with my ideas about conserving electricity. Yet the construction of these plants was very real; they provided more than ten thousand jobs and had the support of everyone and their uncle in the atom-worshipping Tennessee Valley. We needed facts to support any decision to cut back this popular program, and that took time.

The Tennessee Valley public's and TVA distributors' overwhelming support of more nuclear power did not stop them from opposing the rate increase these plants caused, nor did that support inhibit the antinuclear activists (my so-called friends) from demonstrating at TVA public board meetings with anger and tactics that essentially called the board members *murderers*, building more factories that caused deaths. I soon learned that if I kept my cool and didn't respond in anger to these charges, I gained the support of the rest of the public attending the meetings and watching them on TV. I must say when one of the angriest activists once grabbed the microphone and then opened her purse to take out her mirror. I did fear that instead she might have pulled out a gun to shoot me.

The first nuclear plant whose construction we stopped was in Rogersville, Tennessee. This plant's construction had not progressed very far at that point, in 1980. The facts revealed that, even with rapid growth, we really did not need that much additional electricity. And more pertinent, continuing to invest in this nuclear plant would cause rate increases. A decision to close the Rogersville plant would result in laying off one thousand workers. I will never forget the comments of a wife of one of the engineers who would get laid off. At a public meeting I held to explain the decision, she said simply, but with great feeling, "When TVA recruited my husband to come to East Tennessee—a foreign place to me—I didn't object. But we barely got settled in, and now you are firing my husband. What kind of man are you?" I thought I was doing my job of keeping the cost of electricity as low as possible, consistent with protecting the environment. But she sure shook me up.

As the years 1979–1983 unfolded, the nuclear plants became more and more of a problem. The accident at Three Mile Island in Pennsylvania had a major impact on the TVA nuclear plants under construction. We had to incorporate lessons learned about safety from that accident and in effect largely rebuild large parts of the plants. Costs skyrocketed, and more rate increases were necessary to pay the higher costs. Although the Three Mile Island accident added safety concerns to the financial problems in my mind, the opinion leaders in the nuclear-loving Tennessee Valley did not share those concerns.

The facts were becoming crystal clear that TVA was building many more nuclear power plants than needed and their ballooning multibillion-dollar costs were driving up the price of electricity in a region whose economy was built on low-priced power. TVA's consumer efficiency program was reducing the amount of electricity really needed. In addition, the growth in electric usage was far below the prior TVA projections made to justify building all the nuclear reactors.

Despite these facts, TVA's retail distributors stayed dedicated nuclear advocates, and they influenced political leaders in the TVA region to support continued construction. They had almost a religious belief in nuclear power, which continues to this day. The nuclear supporters made the argument that if we didn't finish what we'd started, we'd be wasting a lot of money. And lots of jobs were at stake as well. The truth, of course, was that if we continued, we'd waste lots more and what we spent couldn't be recovered—in the business world, that is called *sunk costs*.

By 1981, it was clear that the remaining cost to finish all nine plants still under construction far exceeded the value to TVA, since we would have plenty of power supply without them. And the escalating costs to complete the plants would mean sizable additional rate increases and, if continued, could even bankrupt TVA. The Freeman Board took on the challenge, and we stopped construction of eight of the ten units under construction when we took office.

With Reagan as president, TVA moved full speed ahead with closing down seven additional large nuclear reactors under construction, in addition to the one in Rogersville, Tennessee, previously shut down. Our success in stopping construction of two reactors in Mississippi, five in Tennessee, and one in Alabama did not come easily. It took a major educational campaign in which our most effective support came not from any antinuclear activist group but from the League of Women Voters, which had been studying TVA. I had previously spent an evening with the league's committee, which was studying TVA, and had satisfied them that our reform agenda was to their liking. Also to my liking was the leader of the league committee, Helen Dey, who became a dear personal friend—a friendship that has lasted the rest of our lives.

The most memorable event in that continuing friendship occurred when we were both in DC during one Christmas season. My two sons, Stan and Roger; my daughter Anita's then husband, Hoppie; Helen; and I were in a car on our way to Atlantic City. Hoppie was driving and was very sober. I was drinking scotch out of a bottle when we saw a giant roadblock up ahead. I, in panic, attempted to pour my scotch out the window. Unfortunately, the window was closed, and the scotch whiskey splashed all over the window and Helen's coat. The car reeked of alcohol, so the cop at the roadblock was amazed to find Hoppie sober. Hoppie never forgave me, but Helen did, and we still laugh at my stupid panic. But again, I digress.

The league hosted a series of meetings to discuss the nuclear plant shutdown issue. They invited business leaders and influential citizens, as well as myself. At these meetings, I laid out the facts and answered questions. In addition, we briefed the editorial boards of the major newspapers and our industrial customers, for whom continued construction would cause rate increases and could wipe out their profits. Of course, Director Freeman and I had the deciding votes, but we were not dictators, and without some local support, Congress could have stopped us through legislation. In the end, the mother love of TVA saved us.

During my confirmation hearing in 1977, Senator Stennis had asked for and received a letter from me promising that I would support the two large nuclear reactors under construction in Mississippi. He had given a speech at the groundbreaking ceremony, which I attended in 1978. The two large reactors in Mississippi were to be the only TVA power plants at the western edge of our service area. At the time I was confirmed, I thought they were needed. It turned out that I was wrong.

By 1981, the post–Three Mile Island costs of these nuclear plants were out of control, and demand for power was well below prior projections. We didn't need to complete them, and if we did, it would require rate increases. So I went to see Senator Stennis, the chairman of the Senate Committee on Appropriations and Armed Services Committee, a powerful senator who could eliminate all of TVA's nonpower programs with the stroke of a pen, so to speak.

The senator's initial reaction was "Mr. Freeman, you made a promise—you gave me your word."

"I know, Senator," I replied, "but these are the facts, which I hope you will consider, and I will await your answer."

The senator shook his head and repeated, "But you gave me your word."

About ten days later, I got a phone call from the senator's chief of staff, who said, "The senator asked me to deliver this message to you. He was in a meeting with President Reagan discussing a major weapons system. He said to the president, 'Don't do what you promised; do what's right.'" I never heard another word from the senator about closing the nuclear plants in Mississippi. The incident reveals the strength of the love and respect the Congresspeople had for TVA who remembered how the valley was before TVA.

But Senator Stennis was just half the problem—the proposed plant, called Yellow Creek, was located in the district of Jamie Whitten, who just happened to chair the appropriations committee in the House of Representatives. I was fortunate in that Chairman Whitten had received three or four letters from people in his district opposing the nuclear plant. That was a lot of letters in his congressional district. And we assured him that the site would be maintained for a future coal-fired plant. He was okay with that result. To my knowledge, no such coal-fired plant has ever been built.

Another incident illustrated the support for this "Socialist" agency in the conservative Tennessee Valley. One day, I got a call from Herb Sanger, TVA's general counsel, who was defending TVA in federal court. Herb said, "Guess what? An attorney from President Reagan's Justice Department showed up in court today and claims that the Justice Department represents TVA under some ancient statute they dug up."

I said, "Don't worry; I know how to stop this. If we don't, we are dead, 'cause the Reagan administration will control us."

I immediately flew to Washington, DC, and went to see Congressman Whitten, the chairman of the appropriations committee, and told him my problem. The congressman said, "You've come to the only person in DC that can fix this, and I know just how to do it." He then went on to tell me that decades prior, House Speaker Cannon put him on the appropriations committee with an understanding that he was to protect TVA's fertilizer research from industry attempts to kill it. Chairman Whitten then said, "I know more about how important TVA's independence is than anyone else in Congress."

He then summoned his chief of staff, Hunter Spillen, into his office and said, "I want you to add permanent law language to the Justice Department appropriations bill forbidding them to spend any money in any way defending the TVA." That language became the law, and we never saw any more of the Reagan Justice Department. The reaction of two powerful valley members of Congress, each of whom had the power to cripple TVA's programs, was typical of the support TVA had and needed to survive a hostile Reagan administration.

TVA was a great supporter of organized labor and all of our construction workers belonged to a union. But we didn't fully realize the power of the United Mine Workers(UMW). In our zeal for cutting costs, TVA awarded a contract for coal to be delivered to TVA's Paradise Power Plant in West Kentucky to a non-union mine. When delivery of the coal began, the UMW workers fired shots at the trucks delivering the coal to the power plant. Falsely assuming that law and order prevailed in west Kentucky, I instructed our attorney to go to federal court and obtain an injunction to stop the coal miners from shooting at the trucks.

The Federal District Judge in West Kentucky handed down an injunction, but to our surprise, he ordered the non-union mine owners to stop delivering coal.

I called my friend Julian Carroll then governor of Kentucky and asked him to call out the National Guard to restore order. He informed me in no uncertain terms that was not going to happen. So we learned a real life lesson. In West Kentucky at that time the United Mine Workers were the law.

Economic development—more good jobs—was still an important part of TVA's mission while I was in charge. I took a serious interest in making sure that TVA gave a high-priority status to carrying out an aggressive program to create more good jobs in the valley. That program was, of course, supported by the other board members and people of the valley. Interestingly, the economic development community, which was skeptical of me in the beginning, became the one crowd that grew more and more supportive of me the longer I was in office. They were really sad when my term expired.

As part of economic development, TVA built a huge computer program and dedicated the staff to preparing studies that connected the attractive features of the valley to the needs of major industries. These studies were crucial in luring industries to locate new factories in the Tennessee Valley. One outstanding example was the Nissan automobile assembly plant built in Tennessee on my watch. What persuaded Nissan to locate in Tennessee was a very detailed study TVA prepared and presented to Nissan. The study proved that the site in Middle Tennessee was an economically attractive location for an automobile assembly plant. We, of course, were sensitive to giving Tennessee governor Lamar Alexander the credit for making the sale. However, TVA's study got Nissan interested in the first place.

I worked personally with Governor Alexander in meeting with numerous prospects for building factories that would create new jobs in the valley. One meeting was with Coors Brewing, a very right-wing outfit. Lamar suggested that I not participate because I might express some of my liberal views and kill the deal. That was fine with me, but I was not unhappy when Coors decided not to locate a brewery in Tennessee. Governor Alexander and I worked well together and always supported each other. Lamar told me that in Republican East Tennessee, he told people that I worked for President Nixon but never mentioned that fact in Democratic Middle Tennessee.

One conflict between TVA and the governor erupted over the Ocoee River. TVA owned an ancient flume into which we withdrew water from the Ocoee River to generate electric power. In order to repair the flume, TVA allowed the water to run down the riverbed instead. All of a sudden, a marvelous rafting experience was created that quickly became a tourist attraction. The problem arose when TVA finished repairing the flume and was about to stop the flow of water down the river and kill the tourist attraction.

Governor Alexander called me and complained. We worked out a compromise to allow the water to flow in the river on weekends when the power demand was lower, thus keeping the rafting alive when most people wanted to enjoy it. We then persuaded Senator Baker to add a little amendment to a federal appropriation bill that reimbursed TVA for its lost revenue. We called that subsidy a *porklet* because it wasn't enough money to be called *pork*.

The Reagan Budget Bureau tried to eliminate TVA's appropriations for nonpower programs, such as fertilizer research, soil conservation, flood control, and the Land Between the Lakes, a small national park. It just took one phone call from me to Senator Baker, then the Republican leader of the Senate, to win that battle. He had his staff tell the Budget Bureau that the senator was too busy "carrying the president's missiles on Capitol Hill to deal with political problems at home the Budget Bureau was causing." The money was immediately reinstated.

With some newspaper and business support in the valley and mother love support from the powerful valley members of Congress, we were able to get away with closing a grand total of eight large nuclear plants while completing one plant by 1984, when my term expired. Perhaps the most important decision Dick Freeman and I made about nuclear power involved the so-called liquid metal fast breeder reactor. This nuclear technology was a central feature of President Nixon's message in 1971 that I drafted. The breeder reactor was the technology that would make nuclear power the truly abundant source of clean energy. It was not perpetual motion, but it did promise to enlarge the nuclear resource to a size that could supply all the planet's energy needs. The demonstration project, located at Oak Ridge, Tennessee, exposed serious safety problems and was billions of dollars over budget.

By 1983, the U.S. Congress refused to appropriate any more money. My friend Senator Baker was the leading proponent of the breeder, and he had an idea on how to save it. The senator invited me to his office for a meeting without naming the subject. As I entered his conference room, I noted pronuclear Senator McClure, Senator Baker's chief of staff, and of course Senator

Baker himself, and I silently said to myself, "This is trouble." And it was.

At the time, President Reagan had already named Charles Dean, a Knoxville native, to the TVA board as its chairman, and I knew Senator Baker had his vote for whatever he was going to ask me. The senator came right to the point—he said correctly that he had never asked me to do anything in all the years I was on the board. And as the Republican Senate majority leader, he was TVA's protector from a Reagan administration that wanted to kill TVA.

He said he wanted TVA to take over the breeder reactor project and complete it as a TVA-financed nuclear power plant. The senator was a friend, and I tried to stave off his request with humor by saying, "Would that mean I would have to testify *in favor* of the project?"

He said, "Dave, I am dead serious."

I said, "Senator, it is a research project whose costs are out of control. There is no way I could justify TVA ratepayers financing a project to the tune of billions of dollars, a project that shows every sign of being a nuclear dream that's not coming true."

To his credit, Senator Baker did not persist. He did not like my answer, but he knew I couldn't be persuaded. He later had a similar meeting with Richard Freeman and, I assume, received a similar answer, although Dick never told me the substance of his conversation with Senator Baker. I believe we put the final nail in the coffin.

Of the breeder reactor project: it ended as a failure shortly thereafter, and there has been no second coming.

Honorary degrees are just that—they kind of go with high office. I still treasure the one I received at Williams College, mainly because of those who were honored at the same event: the congressman Mo Udall, Amory Lovins, and Mr. Anderson, the CEO of Atlantic Richfield—the oil company that opposed the depletion allowance for oil and was in the solar business way back in the early 1980s. I remember getting loud applause from the students when I observed that Amory Lovins could install solar panels on one hundred thousand home roofs, according to a chapter of one his books, but it took me quite a bit longer to put them on real houses in the Tennessee Valley.

As I approached the end of my term, I did very briefly consider running for Congress in the vacant district represented by Al Gore, who had just been elected to the Senate. Al Gore was a friend, and I asked him what he thought. Al, who has a great sense of humor in person, said, "Dave, you've got terrific name recognition, but the problem is that it's mostly bad. You raised the electric rates, and I'm about the only one that hasn't cussed at you for doing it. Furthermore, you are from Chattanooga, not my district. Folks in my district had a hard time accepting me as a native because I went to school in DC when my dad was a senator."

So I dropped the idea. Yet fifteen years later, when I related this episode to Pauline Gore, Al's mother, she said to me, "Al was wrong; we could have gotten you elected easily." Pauline was probably just trying to make me feel good, but she did have very good political judgment of her own. That same evening, I saw then Vice President Gore had his picture on the cover of *Time* magazine for going to Kyoto, Japan, to hammer out a treaty to control greenhouse gases. Pauline told me, "As his mother, I am proud of Al for going to Kyoto, but as his political advisor, I think it was not a good idea."

In my last months at TVA, I took the time to spend several days at TVA's Browns Ferry Nuclear Plant built many years before I became TVA director. The plant had experienced plenty of troubles, including a fire. Nevertheless, the local management constantly complained of undue interference by the Nuclear Regulatory Commission (NRC), which ordered changes at the plant after the Three Mile Island plant in Pennsylvania suffered a near-meltdown.

One afternoon, I asked several of the engineers who managed the plant what they would do differently if I were to get TVA exempted from NRC regulation. This was a purely theoretical question because I had no such intention. The engineers pondered for a few minutes and very cordially said, "We would do about 90 percent or more the same things we are doing, but there would be a big difference—it would be our decisions here in the plant and not some SOB in Washington, DC, telling us how to run our power plant."

That answer was an important insight into how utility operators generally feel about *any* perceived criticism of their work by any outsider. They are "soul brothers" with the machines they build and operate. They really believe it when they say their plant is safe or that it doesn't pollute. In their heart of hearts, newfangled gadgets like solar panels and windmills can't possibly be as good as what they have already built and operated.

The last issue I tackled as TVA director did not work out well. The TVA Act forbade us from paying anyone wages in a year that exceeded what members of Congress got paid. That presented a serious problem for certain skills where we competed with private power companies that paid what it took to attract the talent. For most people, working for a publicly owned company was a form of public service, and modest pay was okay, but not for the skilled operators of nuclear power plants. TVA had become a training center where folks got experience for a few years and then left for higher pay.

We came up with the neat idea of offering a retention bonus. It meant more money in exchange for a promise to stay on the job a number of years. It was legal, but it offended Congress so much that even the mother's love for TVA didn't help. With Senator Sasser in the lead, Congress added a provision in our appropriation bill that outlawed our retention bonus plan. I complained to my friend Senator Hollings, who said, "We are worse on this issue than anything else we do." The great enemy is that the times have really changed. The TVA Act was amended, and TVA's CEO now is paid more than $6 million a year. Maybe I should ask for back pay!

I had an experience in the last two months of my seven years as TVA director that has caused me to be sympathetic to public officials who get caught violating well-meaning but virtually unknown ethic laws. I always remember that there but for an understanding federal prosecutor sit I. What happened was as a director, I routinely approved a grant of money for some project the National Wildlife Federation was carrying out for or with TVA. It wasn't even a project that I proposed or knew much about. The problem was that at the same time, the National Wildlife Federation had offered me a fellowship that paid very little. After I left TVA, I decided not to accept but had not yet rejected it in writing. A federal law makes it a crime to approve money for an outfit that has offered you a job—a good law, which I not only didn't know about but had not actually broken. I was really lucky that the federal prosecutor in East Tennessee saw it my way. He could've put an ugly end to my TVA career.

In some ways, my last day at TVA—May 13, 1984—was the best. Amon Evans and John Seigenthaler, the publisher and editor respectively of the *Tennessean*, the largest newspaper in the valley, invited me to a small private dinner with them in Amon's large wine cellar. There were two surprises. One was a letter from Jimmy Carter, the former president who appointed me—a job-well-done letter that I still cherish. He expressed pleasure at what we had accomplished at TVA under my leadership. The other was a surprise guest—Al Gore.

SINGLE LIFE AS TVA DIRECTOR

TVA was more than a full-time job for me from 1977 to 1984, but I didn't work all the time. I was very happy living alone for the first time in my life. My thirty-year marriage to Marianne effectively ended in 1977, and we finally agreed on the divorce terms in 1980. I had zero interest in getting married again. I was having too much fun being single. Besides, my intense interest in my work also kept me single, until just before my term expired in 1984, when I became engaged to and then married Anne Crawford.

My relationship with Anne Crawford got off to a stumbling start and got more and more complicated as time went on. I first met her at an after-work happy hour where I joined a bunch of TVA employees. She did not work for TVA but had a date with Tom Hebert, a TVA employee I knew, I was instantly smitten and we even danced a bit.

Months later, Hebert was out of the picture, and Anne and I started dating. We had many romantic encounters, but we were like an accordion—every time we grew closer, she would pull away. I was in love with this girl-next-door, brainy, beauty but I did not recognize and admire her artistic talent and interests.

With the benefit of hindsight, I had her up on a pedestal so high that she needed an oxygen mask to breathe. Living up to my picture of her must of seemed like "mission impossible".

Our brief marriage just didn't work; that's all that needs to be said. Anne and I did manage to take a trip together to China while we were marriedin 1984. She didn't much want to go, but I insisted. Knowing we were going to part company, I didn't want her to later regret missing the opportunity. We actually got along rather well on the trip until I got sick and was stuck in a Chinese hospital for six weeks. I do remember that even back in 1984, I had a TV in my Chinese hospital room, which was in a large city then called Quangou. I was a guest of the Chinese government. I recall President Reagan's reelection was covered on Chinese TV for about thirty seconds of the one-hour evening news.

I recovered my health but lost Anne. By the time we got back to Knoxville, she had had enough of me and moved out. We agreed it was such a bad experience that we couldn't be friends. Thirty years later, we came to a different conclusion, but I get ahead of myself.

MOVING ON TO SEATTLE

I felt pretty low when, in December 1984, I was about to move to Seattle, Washington, to consult with a large law firm. My agent, who was renting my condo, called and suggested I come to her office to meet Dr. Mary Jean Smith, a prospective renter. I said I saw no reason to do that and told my agent she could handle it. My agent repeated her plea that I come to her office at once—"It is important that you meet your prospective tenant," she said and then hung up. Exasperated, I went to my agent's office only to find that Dr. Smith was a drop-dead beautiful gal who was a chiropractor by profession. We had dinner that night, and indeed, Mary Jean Smith became a good friend who helped me nurse my wounds from losing Anne Crawford.

I moved to Seattle at the beginning of 1985, having landed a contract to work with a law firm defending the small, publicly owned utilities who suffered large losses when their wholesale supplier caused them to default on their municipal bonds. I was retained to be an expert witness in a trial that never took place. The opponents did take my deposition, and I was told that my testimony helped the parties reach an out-of-court settlement. A year in Seattle was like a vacation compared to the TVA years. In a nutshell, I was bored.

I lived in Seattle for only a year—1985. I adjusted well to living out of the spotlight in large part thanks to the good friends I had in Seattle. Kathy Fletcher—my colleague from the Jimmy Carter think tank in Atlanta in the months before he was elected—and her husband, Ken, treated me as family, as did the partners in the law firm where I worked. I suffered from urinary problems that resulted in an operation during that time. But overall, the year was most pleasant, living right downtown and enjoying Puget Sound and the famous Pike Place Fish Market, where friends would meet every Saturday.

Perhaps most pleasurable of all was a prolonged visit from Dr. Smith, who had rented my Knoxville condo. Dr. Smith, whom I called M. J., was living with me in the summer of 1985 when I realized that we were on different wavelengths—I was still recovering from Anne, and she was getting way too serious for her own good. I leveled with her, and she moved out. Yet we still went on our planned trip to Paris together.

Living in Seattle is so enjoyable that no one ever leaves. In fact, I applied to be the manager of Seattle City Light, the local publicly owned public power system. The mayor at the time was candid in turning me down. He said he didn't want to hire anyone recommended by people like Al Gore, people he would just like to meet. He said he wanted someone who would just run the utility and not make waves. He did not want to worry about getting upstaged by one of his employees. I learned how it felt to be overqualified, but the Freeman luck had not run out, by any means.

ON TO TEXAS

Toward the end of 1985, while I was on vacation, my secretary received a phone call from Bob King, a friend in Austin, Texas, who said that the Lower Colorado River Authority (LCRA), a smaller version of TVA, was in trouble and looking for a new manager. He asked if he could put my name in the pot. She called to relay the message, and I said yes and soon went off to Texas for my next adventure. As comfortable as life was in Seattle, I could not resist another chance to advance my ideas about energy efficiency and renewable energy in the very red state of Texas.

In January 1986, after I was hired, I moved to Austin and became the general manager of the LCRA. The LCRA is a water and power agency, a little TVA. The LCRA serves the Texas Hill Country in a doughnut shape around, but not including, Austin. It sells electricity at wholesale to co-ops and cities and preserves water quality in the Lower Colorado River. It can correctly be called the son of TVA. Lyndon Johnson was instrumental in creating the agency; that was his early claim to fame and fortune.

I found life quite different in Texas. As part of the interview process for the LCRA job, they insisted I take an IQ test, which I passed. The next step was to visit each of the fifteen LCRA board members at their homes throughout the state. This process revealed that you had to be quite wealthy and influential to be on the LCRA board. For example, we had difficulty finding the house of one board member who lived in Wharton County. When I inquired at a gasoline station, the attendant replied, "Well, he owns about half the county and has both a his and hers Rolls-Royce in his garage. I think you can find him."

Bob King, who connected me to the LCRA, was my friend in Austin when I first arrived. But I already had other friends, like Robert Floyd, an architect who was also a former TVA employee. Over the years, Robert became one of the very best male friends I ever had. He helped me decide to purchase a very beautiful home in Austin that I could afford to own only because I persuaded the LCRA to loan me the three-hundred-thousand-dollar purchase price and pay interest at their low cost.

I no longer walked among the wounded over Anne, and I plunged into an active dating life in Austin, a much more fun town than Knoxville, Tennessee. The music, food, and women were all good fun. I played a lot of tennis and ate a lot of barbeque. And with the help of Bob King and Robert Floyd, I made lots of other good friends.

As I took office at the LCRA, I found the outfit was in a heap of trouble. The agency had just received a report by a former district attorney who had investigated the agency at the LCRA board's request. It stated that the staff had misled the board in their presentation on the design of a conveyer belt for its lignite mine. More sensational was the revelation that one of the contractors had treated staff to sexual favors. But worst of all, major LCRA customers planned to build their own power plant and stop purchasing electricity from the LCRA. As a result of the scandals, I had to fire the most popular manager in the company and a few others as well. I also had to make peace with our customers. With the benefit of experience and luck, I was able to bring the family back together and clean house.

I learned the value of symbolic actions that speak the language of reform loud and clear. One very popular Texas state senator, John Sharp, was a leader in beating up the LCRA as an outfit that spent money like drunken sailors. I ordered all our managers to turn in their American Express credit cards. I cut them all in half, put them in a large paper bag, and presented them to Senator Sharp. He then traveled far and wide, showing off that paper bag and claiming he had cleaned up the LCRA.

I had an early meeting with our largest customers, the Pedernales and Bluebonnet Cooperatives. I agreed that the LCRA would buy out their investment in the power plant they planned to build (about $7 million in studies), and they agreed to forget about leaving the family and help me make peace with all our customers. It worked.

Perhaps my greatest success at the LCRA was that I stopped the opening of a lignite mine that the LCRA board had already approved and for which large cranes that you could see from fifty miles away had already been purchased and erected. Over a three-year period, with the help of some new faces on the board, I was able to stop that lignite mine from opening. By doing so, we saved a beautiful part of Fayette County, Texas, from being destroyed. At the same time, we stopped the LCRA from using lignite, which has half the heating power of coal and is twice as dirty—in other words, it's an environmental disaster. Whenever I get discouraged, I remember I can always go back and get a big hug from some of those Fayette County farmers, good folks who helped win that fight.

Closing the lignite mine left the LCRA with the need for a long-term fuel supply for the large coal-fired power plant in Fayette County that the LCRA operated, which it co-owned with the City of Austin. We had stopped taking coal under a high-priced contract that we sued over, claiming that the coal was sold to us with misleading facts that amounted to fraud. We negotiated a much-lower-cost coal contract and settled the lawsuit with the high-priced contractor. We obtained low-sulfur coal delivered to the LCRA plant in Texas from Wyoming for less than two cents per kilowatt-hour, the lowest cost of any power plant in Texas. We initiated energy efficiency and solar programs at the LCRA, but frankly, they were not a big deal since we did not sell electricity at retail and we had no control over the cities and coperatives, who were our customers.

A major challenge involved water and water quality. The lakes formed by LCRA dams were getting polluted by the runoffs from surrounding farms and residents. We were determined to preserve the lakes and achieved results that, looking back, seem incredible. The key to our success was a film narrated by Walter Cronkite, the famous TV newsman, who had a daughter with a home on one of the LCRA lakes. The film we made showed how polluted the lakes would become if we didn't take action. As a result of it, we succeeded in adopting and implementing restrictions on pollution runoff from all lakeside property.

The ordinance the LCRA adapted required that lakeshore landowners install filters and other devices to control the polluted runoff otherwise going into the lakes. Imposing land-use restrictions in the red state of Texas may seem impossible today, but we actually did it in 1987, and those restrictions are maintained to this day.

The LCRA had quite a dispute with the City of Austin when they attempted to build a large water-pumping station on the shores of one of our lakes that would have drained it dry during the summer recreation months. There was much concern in Austin at the time about a nuclear power plant that the City of Austin owned, in part because its costs were causing electric rate increases. So I labeled the pumping plant a *water nuke*, and we succeeded in killing the project.

Austin, Texas, had a serious interest in water quality, and we were able to impose pollution control standards on the Lower Colorado River that were more stringent than even in California. I firmed up the LCRA's rights to Colorado River water by helping the authority win litigation over water rights. And I initiated the first total cleanup of that famed river. We had huge rallies, bringing out people to pick up junk along the riverbanks. We made strides in water quality. I forced one sewage treatment plant that was spewing its discharge into one of our lakes to spread the effluent, or sewage, over the land for use as a fertilizer.

The LCRA provided lots of water from the Lower Colorado River to the rice farmers at a price that was a giveaway. We even operated a canal from the river to the rice farms. We were losing money big time on the water going to the rice farms, so I proposed a modest price increase just to cover the LCRA's cost of maintaining the canal from the river to their farms. When I discussed the increase at a meeting with the rice farmers, they acted as if the world was coming to an end.

I reacted by calmly stating that they left me no choice other than to report back to my board that we would just stop maintaining and operating the canals taking the water to their farms. The LCRA is a nonprofit public agency, and we simply could not afford to use money from other water customers to pay for deliveries for the rice farmers. The small increase I proposed went into effect without any more fuss.

At the LCRA, I was a manager reporting to a fifteen-person board of directors, a very different job from being the all-powerful chairman of the TVA board. I needed to always count to eight, but I still had to lead because a fifteen-person board, by nature, could only say yes or no to what I proposed. The governor appointed the LCRA board. By custom, it was then bipartisan and not political, but it was made up of prominent citizens who were mostly intelligent, conservative, and fair-minded. I benefited from their anger at the way one or two narrow-minded members treated my environmentally progressive proposals. The majority adopted them even if they were stronger than what they would have proposed out of a sense of support and fairness.

At the LCRA, I had my first experience with managing a utility that was regulated. The Public Utility Commission of Texas controlled the LCRA's rates for electricity. Being subject to regulation was a learning experience of how money is wasted because of regulatory red tape. The regulatory process can inhibit a good utility, even though regulation is needed to put a lid on how much a monopoly can charge. Once, when I wanted to refund to customers funds that the LCRA overcollected during a cold month, the Texas Public Utility Commission was about to say no because it would embarrass the private utilities who were not refunding any money to their customers. I had to appear personally to get their reluctant approval.

I learned the value of informal contracts with employees and not just sitting in my office and getting input only from top management. For example, the manager at our large coal-fired power plant in Fayette County, Texas, was inept, and we needed to replace him. A female employee who drove me around knew all the guys in the plant and called my attention to Doug Pilant, a person everyone liked who turned out to be great as the new manager.

I learned to deal with life-and-death issues involving employees. One example was our general counsel, who became an acute alcoholic. He refused to go into rehab even though he was no longer able to do his job. I checked with his girlfriend, who confirmed what I feared: that his doctors were saying he was literally killing himself. I didn't have evidence I could make public to fire him, and I didn't want to do that. So I deliberately lied to him—promised him I'd keep his job open if he went to rehab. He did, and I didn't keep my word because even after rehab, he couldn't do the job. He appealed to the LCRA board, and they backed me up. He lived another thirty years, so I think I did the right thing.

John Scanlan was a very wealthy LCRA board member who helped recruit me and was initially a strong supporter and good personal friend. I nursed him through a divorce, and we played lots of tennis together. It all fell apart because I wrote a letter to support a local water system at the request of the board president, also a good friend, and John thought that was a mistake. He never forgave me. I tried to apologize to him—he refused to even talk to me. I was wrong to have written the letter, but John Scanlan expected perfection. I just didn't measure up to that standard. Another LCRA board member came into my office one day and asked that I hire him to work for the LCRA. I politely told him that this meeting just hadn't taken place. I never heard anything more from him about a job.

I got a good insight into Texas politics from a friend from rural East Texas who was a leader in the Texas legislature. He was a very conservative Democrat. In 1988, when Dukakis was running for president against Bush Sr., he told me if Dukakis had come to his district and "stood up in the open end of a pickup truck with a shotgun in his hand and wearing a hunting shirt and yelled, 'You're damn right, I am liberal—anyone want to make something of that?'" he would have carried the district. How you look and talk matter in Texas.

I had actually had a small exposure to presidential politics earlier in 1988 when one of my friends, Ed Wendler, and I put together a Texas political road map for Al Gore, who was running in the Democratic presidential primary. We hosted then Senator Gore in Austin. It was his first presidential run.

Life in Austin was good. Folks were friendly, and I made a number of true friends who remain close to this day. I enjoyed life there so much that my bachelorhood ended at about the time I was preparing for my next adventure in California. I lost my bachelorhood when my late friend Ed Wendler and I attended the Democratic convention in Atlanta in 1988 and stayed in an apartment that our friend Jim Hightower had rented for us. We attended the Texas party the night the governor Ann Richards, who was state treasurer at the time, gave her famous speech about Bush Sr. having been born with a "silver foot in his mouth."

At the party, I found myself dancing with a gal named Suzanne who was a reporter for a newspaper in Marble Falls, a community near Austin. A dispute over who picked who up has never been decided. But it is a fact that that our "dance," in a few short weeks, led to her moving into my to-die-for redwood home in Austin and to our marriage just before leaving Austin for Sacramento, California.

By 1989, we had pretty well cleaned up and resolved the urgent problems facing the LCRA, and I had succeeded in alienating the mostly conservative members of my board. I was by no means bored, but a steady-as-you-go manager was what they really wanted, and I was open to another adventure. That adventure came from Sacramento, which by 1990 had achieved the distinction of having the worst utility in America.

CALIFORNIA, HERE I COME

When I first asked Alex Radin, my lifelong friend from Chattanooga and the head of the American Public Power Association, about the offer from the Sacramento Municipal Utility District (SMUD), he said, "Dave, you've had a good run. If you take that job, it will ruin your reputation. They've fired five managers in the last six years." That comment, frankly, made me even more eager to take the job because I knew from experience that no utility can't be fixed if you have the authority to fix it and some time.

When I called up Dave Cox, a SMUD board member, just to get his opinion about me, he asked me, "Dave, do you have a good jobin Texas?"

I answered, "Yes."

He said, "If I were you, I'd keep it. This is not a place to expect to do any good." And he voted against hiring me. The SMUD board vote to hire me was 3–2, not exactly a ringing vote of confidence.

Ed Smeloff was the SMUD board chairman who actively recruited me and worked hard to persuade two other board members to agree to hire me. He had led the successful fight to close SMUD's Rancho Seco nuclear plant and shared my ideas on efficiency and renewable energy. He told me that he had reached out to President Carter to check up on me and that the former president had personally called him on the phone to say good things about me.

SMUD really was dysfunctional. The public anger came home with me when my wife, Suzanne, and I were looking at a home to purchase in Sacramento right after I was hired. The next-door neighbors came over to chat with us, but upon finding that I was the new general manager at SMUD, one of them said, "I hate SMUD," and walked away.

I interviewed people on the street, and eight out of ten said they hated SMUD. One said SMUD were crooks, and another said, "I just pay my bill." The editor of the *Sacramento Bee* told me that in the previous twelve months, his paper had run more than four hundred articles about SMUD, all unfavorable. "If you can just get SMUD out of my newspaper, I would be happy. Folks are just tired of reading about how SMUD has screwed up."

SMUD's Rancho Seco nuclear power plant supplied 50 percent of SMUD's power. It broke down regularly and was the cause of increasing electric rates. By a vote of the people just before I arrived on the scene, it was decided that SMUD could no longer operate the plant. The nearby private utility, Pacific Gas and Electric, had already launched a campaign to take over SMUD.

Troublingly, the board members had engaged in excessive micromanagement by going around the general manager and directing staff. I was experienced enough to negotiate a contract requiring them to pay me for at least three years, even if they fired me. At the first board meeting, I publicly told the board to refrain from speaking to any staff member but me and to recognize that I wasn't going to feel obligated to do what they said unless the contract was adopted during a public board meeting.

By the time I became SMUD general manager, I had learned the essential lesson that a new GM has to visibly take charge in the first few weeks, or else he or she will fade into the woodwork. I therefore came on pretty strong. One of the most visible examples of SMUD waste was their purchasing a whole bunch of fancy clothing for the employee operators in the control room of the then-closed nuclear plant and expensive furniture, such as brass-plated trash cans. I therefore held an auction to "get rid of the waste and get some of the wasted money back." I persuaded local TV to cover the auction. It was a symbolic act to help create a visible impression that we were, in fact, cleaning house.

I also took early steps to win over the rank-and-file employees. When I discovered that when an employee got injured on the job, they first gave him or her a drug test, I abolished that rule on the spot. I instituted flextime so employees could work four ten-hour days. And I held attitude-adjustment parties after work at a nearby park where the utility provided hot dogs and beer. That way, I learned what was really going on at the company.

Perhaps the biggest early break was that I persuaded a major local TV channel to follow me all day one day, and they ran seven to eight minutes of the footage on the evening news. As a visible economy measure, I had ordered all the managers who had company cars to turn them in, and one manager had refused. The TV reporter asked me what I said when he refused. I said, "Bye-bye." SMUD customers then knew I was serious about cost cutting and that there really was a new sheriff in town.

I took charge, and the divided board really had no choice but to back me up. It took positive action, not just words, to reform and revitalize SMUD. And we went to work right away. First, we launched the most massive efficiency program in the nation to offset the loss of the nuclear plant. We called it a *conservation power plant.*

We initiated efficiency measures that offset all the growth in the SMUD system in the 1990s. We formed a partnership with an existing nonprofit called the Tree Foundation to plant a million trees in Sacramento in the next ten years. And those trees were planted mostly to shade homes and reduce the need for air-conditioning as part of our energy efficiency program. We built a number of small cogeneration plants adjunct to industries that utilized waste heat from the power plants.

The major challenge was to replace the power from the dead nuclear plant without raising the rates that consumers paid. Through conservation, purchased power, and cost cutting, we were okay, except the NRC rules required that we spend a billion dollars to decommission the plant, or tear it apart, and since we shut it down well before its license expired, we didn't have enough money in the fund to do the decommissioning. We faced a large rate increase that could have prompted another public vote that might have reopened the nuclear plant.

I knew there was only one answer—I flew to Washington, DC, and persuaded the NRC to allow us to delay the decommissioning until a decade later, when the trust fund for that purpose would be large enough to pay for it. I dodged that bullet. I might add that I don't believe a dead nuke should be torn apart. Doing so exposes the workers to radiation and sends the highly radioactive pieces off to shallow graves that will be dangerous for hundreds of years. It's a large waste of money. The dead plant should be left alone, perhaps encased in concrete, as a visible tombstone.

We faced another serious problem with the nuclear plant—the vote of the people required SMUD to stop operating the plant but left open the option of SMUD selling or leasing the plant to another operator. And I faced an offer from Electricite de France, a giant French nuclear company. I worked with Bob Mulhallen, an activist who was a leader of the shutdown campaign. He informed the French company that they would encounter the likes of World War III if they persisted with their offer. The offer then just died, and Rancho Seco was dead for good.

In short, we kept the lights on, the rates level, and the bills lower through efficiency, and we let the dead nuclear power plant rest in peace. I had voted to close nuclear plants at TVA and bury the SMUD plant on the basis of excessive costs. I was already a nuclear skeptic, but a visit to Chernobyl, the site of a nuclear disaster in the Ukraine, instilled a serious fear of nuclear power in me.

We were solar pioneers back in the early 1990s. SMUD built solar panels on people's roofs. We only asked our customers to "lend us their roof"; we paid for and installed the solar panels. There was a functioning one-megawatt solar array near the dead Rancho Seco power plant. A photograph went around the world of the dead nuke in the background and the solar array in the foreground. I initiated major energy efficiency programs at the New York Power Authority (NYPA).

We also demonstrated electric cars and built a wind farm with the wind technology available in the 1990s. We had an electric car program way back in 1996. We located a pool of electric cars at subway train stops in the suburbs. Consumers who took the train to and from New York City could use an electric car overnight for the trip home and back from the train station. It worked. The turbines failed, yet we were wise enough to buy the windy land, and today, that wind farm is powered by modern turbines and serves SMUD and its customers quite well. We were fortunate that the press seemed hungry for a positive story from SMUD now, in contrast to in the past, and we got coverage of symbolic acts that showed we had tightened our belt and gotten our house in order.

Amazingly, things settled down so that in a year's time, SMUD changed from an incompetent villain to an agency gaining serious respect in the community. And Pacific Gas and Electric gave up on their attempt to put SMUD out of business. But I can't help remembering the mindset that pervaded in the early months that was epitomized by an incident that happened after I gave a luncheon speech to a major Rotary Club in downtown Sacramento. As I walked out of the hall, I overheard two of the members chatting. One said, "You know that new fellow sounded pretty good," and the other one said, "They all sound good on the way in."

Yet even after we had calmed the waters, so to speak, the SMUD board could not stand success. As I developed the smaller decentralized power projects and efficiency measures to replace the nuclear plant, two of the board members who hired me came to my office and urged that I recommend converting the dead nuclear plant into a large gas-fired plant, a proposal made by a Michigan company. I did not include the project they recommended in my proposed development package presented to the board because the smaller projects I proposed were lower in cost and created more jobs in Sacramento.

Mr. Smeloff, the board president who recruited me, berated me at the board meeting and suggested the board hire a consultant and get another opinion. He thought he would get the board to approve the large gas-fired plant. I had to remind him privately that my contract stated the board couldn't hire a consultant without my approval and we didn't need to waste money on a consultant. The board then approved our proposal for smaller, decentralized plants. The public solidly backed my slogan—"Don't put all our eggs in one basket again"—suggested by a PR friend, Richie Ross.

That incident persuaded me that SMUD needed to have a larger board so that one or two board members could not intimidate the general manager. I went to my friends in the legislature without telling the board and persuaded the Sacramento representative Lloyd Connelly to introduce legislation to enlarge the board from five to seven members. The existing board members who had hired me opposed the legislation, but nevertheless, the California legislature enacted it. There was a clear threat of a veto since the Republican Governor Wilson almost automatically vetoed any bill sponsored by the liberal Lloyd Connelly.

There was a crucial meeting with the governor's staff to decide whether he would veto or sign the legislation. At the meeting, Governor Wilson's staff asked me if the liberals on the SMUD board were behind this bill. I said, "No, they sent you a letter opposing it." That satisfied Governor Wilson, so Mr. Smeloff and Wendy Reid, the two board members who opposed the bill, helped get the governor to sign it. That reform has proved to be very valuable in that there have been no problems of micromanagement by the SMUD board ever since.

I made a conscious effort to recruit qualified minorities for top jobs at SMUD. As part of an affirmative action program, I recruited James Shelby, an African American, who reported directly to me and led our minority economic development efforts. Shelby later became leader of the Sacramento Urban League. We built a strong working relationship with the Urban League, the Black Chamber of Commerce, and the Women's Civic Improvement Club to bring more African Americans and other minority groups up the competitive ladder within SMUD.

SMUD's new headquarters office building that we built symbolized our affirmative action. I stayed determined that a rainbow coalition would construct this beautiful building. I was told it couldn't be done because there weren't enough minority contractors available. I met with the general contractor who won the award and told him, "The only way this building will get built is if there is a tremendous array of diverse talent." He went out and found female and minority subcontractors. SMUD's new headquarters was built by the most diverse workforce in Sacramento history. It was also completed on time and under budget.

I believe that my tenure at SMUD perhaps had the most lasting positive impact of any of the jobs I have held. SMUD has continued to lead efficiency and renewable energy work, and there has been no problem of individual board members politicizing the agency with micromanagement.

My wife, Suzanne, became very active in the Democratic Party as soon as we moved to Sacramento. Indeed, she was the Sacramento leader for Bill Clinton's presidential campaign from 1991 to 1992. Bill Clinton was my friend from my days at TVA, when he was the governor of Arkansas. In Sacramento in 1991, while campaigning for president, he spotted me in the crowd and said, "I don't usually admit being friends with utility executives, but I want everyone to know that Dave Freeman in the audience here is a good friend of mine." That remark caused lots of folks, including me, to believe I was going to Washington when Bill Clinton was elected president. But that didn't happen. President Clinton named Hazel O'Leary his energy secretary. I was told that Vice President Gore called me overqualified to be an assistant secretary. Energy Secretary O'Leary didn't want anyone in her department who knew the president better than she did.

Suzanne was much more successful in her political endeavors. We hosted Al Gore's father and his wife, Pauline, when they campaigned for Clinton–Gore in Sacramento. Suzanne and I spent the entire day with Senior Senator Gore and his wife. As a result of Suzanne's influence, she and I were both elected delegates to the

Democratic convention where Clinton and Gore were nominated. I will always remember how excited we were the day Ross Perot pulled out of the race. As a result of Suzanne's efforts, we both got invited to a White House dinner after Bill Clinton became president.

I must admit a tremendous hunger for challenges. For example, in 1994, when SMUD was no longer in trouble and our emphasis on efficiency and renewables was widely supported and going strong, I couldn't sit still and was looking for a new adventure. So I decided that, since I was quite popular in the community, I would run for the California State Assembly as a Democrat in a seat that could go either way. I lined up my friend Richie Ross who was a skilled campaign manager. We decided that we would base the campaign on the theme that in the legislature, I would "follow the money in state government and try to get the government to do more with less." Our theme showed I would make lemonade out of lemons. We bought a whole bunch of lemons to hand out during rallies. And then there was a phone call from a friend named Peter Bradford about New York.

NEW YORK, NEW YORK

The NYPA, which Franklin Roosevelt created when he was governor of New York before he became president, was in a bit of trouble. The president of the NYPA got caught using the company airplane to go to his country home on weekends. Governor Cuomo was looking for a replacement. My friend Peter Bradford brought my name to his attention, and the governor's emissaries called me to ask if I was interested in the job. I was intrigued but torn between running for the California State Assembly and taking on yet another utility repair job.

My wife, Suzanne, had a lifelong ambition to go to the Columbia University School of Journalism in New York City and was agreeable to my taking the job located there. That tipped the balance of my decision, despite the fact that the NYPA board was more than a little miffed that the governor was, in effect, telling them whom to hire. Indeed, the deal almost fell apart during a phone interview when one of the NYPA board members, whose vote was crucial, tried to get me to agree that the board had to approve my management team. I said no, and he backed off but was very unhappy that I took the job.

We moved to New York City and rented a large apartment on the West Side of Manhattan. My office was at Fiftieth and Broadway. I had a car and chauffeur. We were in the Big Apple, and Suzanne was achieving her dream of attending the Columbia School of Journalism.

I knew good and well I had to take charge in a hurry and very visibly, or I would be hamstrung by a resentful board of directors. I was able to take a major action within days of arriving on the scene. Hydro-Quebec had proposed building a dam in Canada that would flood the homeland of a large number of natives who had been living the same lifestyle for hundreds of years. Robert Kennedy Jr. and many others had been fighting the dam for years. Essential to building the dam were contracts for the purchases of hydropower the dam would create, which the NYPA and the Consolidated Edison Company (Con Edison) in New York were on the verge of signing. If the contracts did not get approved, the dam would not be built.

I had to appear before the New York State Legislature about this issue a week after I took over as president of the NYPA. After wisely clearing my decision in advance with Governor Cuomo and my NYPA board, I announced that the NYPA was rejecting the contract because the price was too high and the environmental damage was too great. Never before, or after, that event did I get the kind of standing, cheering response to my testimony that I did then from the audience and the legislators.

A couple of days later, in a prominent article in the *New York Times*, I was asked why Con Edison had not also rejected the contract, and I was quoted as saying, "They are not as environmentally sensitive as NYPA." A few days later, Con Edison rejected the contract also, and the dam died. Robert Kennedy Jr. has been my friend ever since.

I learned quickly how important the NYPA's low-cost electricity was for the economy of Upstate New York. I also learned how tight knit the workforce was in those fairly remote locations, such as Niagara Falls. The lesson got driven home when the entire workforce at the NYPA's Niagara Falls hydro station—a really big dam with a very small workforce—was in rebellion because, in a misguided cost-cutting effort, my predecessor laid off two longtime employees. Mind you, the Niagara Falls dam was a huge cash cow for the NYPA. We were selling electricity for one cent per kilowatt-hour and making huge profits. I became an instant hero, both with the employees and with their union by reinstating those two jobs at Niagara.

The NYPA had a program called Juice for Jobs under which large aluminum plants and other energy-intensive plants received electricity for one cent per kilowatt-hour in exchange for promising to maintain a certain number of good-paying jobs. The large hydroelectric plants built seventy years ago in New York, the Tennessee Valley, and the Pacific Northwest have the lowest-cost renewable energy today. Free fuel power, like solar and wind, can play the same role tomorrow.

A personally important event during my NYPA gig was my recruitment of Angelina Galiteva to work for the NYPA. It was important not so much because of her excellent and passionate work for energy efficiency and renewable energy, but more important, because she became a friend for the rest of my life. She followed me back to California at various jobs from 1996 to 2001 and has been a best friend ever since. Actually, I did not recruit her. Her law school professor Dick Ottinger, a former congressman, told me I had to hire her since she was the best student he had ever taught. Angelina really interviewed *me*, and I passed her test.

One serious problem I faced was the NYPA's nuclear power plant called Indian Point Unit 3 on the Hudson River, no more than sixty miles from New York City. It was down for repairs for a couple of years, and the workforce seemed unable to fix it. I had negotiated with Governor Cuomo before I took the job that if I really needed an expert, I could hire one person at a very high salary. I therefore hired Mr. Cahill, who had been in charge of building that power plant and was now semiretired. I figured if anyone could fix the plant, he could. And he did.

I believe I played a useful role by speaking to the workforce. I was very blunt. I told them I had voted to shut down eight nuclear power plants in the Tennessee Valley, and I would have no trouble closing this plant down if the employees continued the pattern of breaking the rules and screwing things up. But with Mr. Cahill's leadership, I was willing to give it one more shot at getting it right. In any event, the plant returned to service. Years after I left, the NYPA sold the plant to another utility for many, many millions of dollars. After the Fukushima accident in Japan in 2011, I have grave doubts about my 1995 decision to fix the plant only sixty miles from New York City. I made a mistake.

The NYPA was a very profitable nonprofit public power agency. It really did not have any serious problems. The job was easy compared to my jobs at SMUD and TVA. I arrived on the scene at the NYPA in late 1995 and was really just beginning to rock-and-roll with the new programs when, a year later, I was diagnosed one Friday afternoon in December with blocked arteries to the heart. I was kept at New York–Presbyterian Hospital over the weekend and had quadruple-bypass open-heart surgery on Monday. I recovered and was back at work in February 1996.

Later that year, to my surprise, Governor Cuomo was defeated for reelection. I submitted my resignation, assuming Governor Pataki wanted his own person for the job. I must add that the new governor pursued the energy efficiency and other clean-tech programs I started with enthusiasm. To this day, the NYPA plays an active role in progress toward clean energy. It is a very strong utility financially, with two large hydro projects, the Niagara and St. Lawrence Dams, and ownership of much of the transmission system in New York State. The NYPA sells its power at wholesale to cities, co-ops, and major industrial customers upstate that would not be located there if not for the low-cost NYPA power.

After I left the NYPA, Suzanne and I felt lost in a fast-paced big city. We did not have the unifying interest in political action that bonded us in Sacramento. Even before my open-heart surgery, her interests in school and church left me feeling distant. Even our parenting of her two sons, Brian and Kevin, caused more anxiety than togetherness because she was the decider and I was just an advisor who felt left out.

After I left the NYPA, I sort of goofed off in New York City. My coworker at the NYPA and friend, Angelina Galiteva, and I formed a company called Sunlight Power, which sought to bring solar panels to the more than one billion people in Africa and Asia who didn't have any electricity at all. The idea makes even more sense today, with the dramatically lower cost of solar technology. But even back in 1996, solar panels just for lighting were economic compared to the cost of the kerosene people used. The problem was we couldn't get investors interested in becoming a solar utility because of the uncertainty in distant lands of getting paid for the solar power. But it is a fact that a small solar power and battery combination can provide electricity for lighting and a computer that would dramatically improve the standard of living of 1.2 billion folks. They remain blacked out. It is an unfulfilled challenge that we can overcome with modern technology, but the market doesn't reach those folks.

CALIFORNIA, HERE I COME—AGAIN

What happened next was another life-changing phone call. This time, the call was to go back to California. In late 1996, Chairman Fessler of the California Public Utilities Commission and Chuck Imbright, the president of the California Energy Commission, called, speaking on behalf of the governor, Pete Wilson. They wanted me to come home and take responsibility for implementing the newly enacted electric power deregulation legislation. I asked, "Why me?" They stated I had the confidence of the privately owned and publicly owned utilities. My title would be *trustee*, and my job would involve implementing the law that created the independent system operator (ISO), the entity to manage the electric power grid in California, and a power exchange where electricity could be bought and sold in the marketplace.

The offer from California came at a time when my marriage to Suzanne had run out of gas. After my open-heart surgery, I felt Suzanne was frightened and she wanted me to just stay home. Her career was growing and centered in New York City. She had no interest in moving back to California. We did not end our marriage, but just like when I left Marianne to lead TVA in Tennessee, I moved to San Francisco with our marriage in trouble but not yet ended.

My new gig was a most unusual job. My contract was with the California Public Utilities Commission (CPUC). My job was to create the ISO, an outfit that would manage the California electric power grid made up of transmission lines owned and previously operated by individual utilities. In addition, we created a power exchange, where electricity could be bought and sold at wholesale. In a short period of time, it became apparent the power exchange was not needed, and it thus failed.

I was paid a salary and expenses that included a nice apartment in San Francisco on Telegraph Hill. I had an office downtown overlooking the San Francisco Bay. I was told that if I followed the recommendations of an advisory committee made up of utility and consumer leaders, no one could successfully challenge my decisions. But if I rejected their advice, I was on my own. I quickly developed a procedure for me to discuss issues with the advisory committee in advance so they would recommend the actions that were okay with me. We worked together, and I would then enthusiastically approve their recommendations. And we did get things done in a timely fashion.

Creating a new organization was a new sort of challenge. I faced the task of physically building the infrastructure, buildings, and highly technical machines and hiring people. The most interesting and challenging part was hammering out the rules under which the ISO would operate the California transmission grid. I knew very little about the technical challenges we faced as I tried to mediate between the conflicting policy views of the utility folks and the consumers. I learned to be a good listener and much more of a diplomat than I ever had been before.

As trustee, I made the first filing to the Federal Energy Regulatory Commission, spelling out the basic rules to govern what became the California Independent System Operator, before its board was even appointed. That filing, which the Federal Energy Regulatory Commission approved, determined how the new ISO would control the power grid in California. The filing was a major understanding that required some $4 million in legal fees to a British firm that did the detailed work based on their experience with deregulation in Great Britain. We were exploring new ground in America. In addition to the basic rules, the filing continued the ISO's plan for a statewide grid on which electricity could flow all over the state. And it gave the ISO the authority to build any needed transmission lines that were not being built. (The power exchange was also started in a timely fashion, but it did not have a very long life; it ceased operations.) The ISO continues as a critical, successful member of the energy family in California.

As trustee, I became aware that the deregulation system enacted by the California legislature was subject to manipulation by companies that wanted to create false shortages to get higher prices. Unfortunately, I had no power to change the basic rules for regulation of wholesale prices. The die had been cast in the law enacted by the state legislature and signed by the governor. I did hire an expert on power system manipulation named Dr. Wilson, but his recommendations could not change the deregulation system that California had already adopted. In all honesty, I didn't foresee just how bad it would become during the energy crisis of 2000–2001.

My personal life as trustee in San Francisco was great. I could walk to work and hike in the beautiful areas north of San Francisco near the beach on the weekends. I remained married to Suzanne, but we saw very little of each other. I spent a lot of free time with my friend Angelina Galiteva. It didn't help my marriage when Suzanne visited me in San Francisco and found out that Angelina was working for me. It was only guilt by association because Angelina and I were friends, nothing more. I did understand why Suzanne was suspicious. Frankly, I didn't care.

My work as trustee was essentially completed in 1997, when the permanent board of directors of the ISO was put in place. The California ISO then became a viable organization.

LOS ANGELES

My next job popped up like magic. Ralph Cavanagh, a California friend at the Natural Resources Defense Council, a prominent environmental group, introduced me to Ruth Galanter, the LA city council member who oversaw the Los Angeles Department of Water and Power (LADWP). She and mostly Brian D'Arcy, the head of the Department of Water and Power (DWP) union, persuaded a reluctant Mayor Riordan to appoint me the general manager of the LADWP in 1997.

Mayor Riordan was a fairly conservative Republican, and he really wanted to hire someone from the private power sector. His problem was the job didn't pay enough to attract any of them and the liberal LA city council wouldn't approve a higher salary for the general manager. In a sense, I got the job because I was the low bidder.

My friend and coworker Angelina Galiteva accepted my offer to be my green person at the DWP and went to LA with me. She was *not* my girlfriend, but through no fault of her own, she cost me a real girlfriend of mine, Mary Aubry, who was once my executive secretary at TVA and is now an accomplished attorney.

Mary had promised to visit me in LA the first weekend I arrived, I thought, but she didn't show, and when I called, I couldn't reach her. The next weekend, Angelina and I, as friends, went to a movie on a Friday night. Afterward, I went to my new home alone. The next morning, I woke up to see Mary in my living room. She had arrived while I was at the movies, and finding no one at my home, she crawled through an open window and went to sleep in another bedroom. The mistake I made was asking Angelina to join us the next night, as I found out later on that Mary decided to drop me because she wrongly assumed I was two-timing her with Angelina.

As I took office in LA, I found a strong fear that the DWP might go bankrupt due to competition from other power companies under deregulation. Again, I was able to take some early actions that generated widespread support. I took advantage of that fear and launched a massive cost-cutting program and asserted that would beat the competition. Everyone soon learned there was a new sheriff in charge.

My first step was to kill a rate increase that the utility staff was proposing. That action really impressed the businessman Mayor Riordan, who was worried that I was a spendthrift liberal, which I was. I discovered that the DWP had a thousand more employees than we needed. I then learned that the DWP retirement system was overfunded. Therefore, I offered employees an early retirement option in cooperation with the union, which resulted in the reduction of the more than one thousand folks we didn't need, some 10 percent of the workforce.

The leader of the large union, Brian D'Arcy, agreed to the early retirement package we offered employees since the people targeted for retirement were the engineers he didn't then represent. I then casually said, "Don't we need to offer it to your people too? Brian, you'll look bad if we don't." He agreed and, as a result, lost one thousand of his members—and never forgave me.

I decided that my only choice, considering the restraints imposed by LA city government, was to take Mayor Riordan's advice: not to ask permission but to ask forgiveness. I was far along in implementing the early retirement program before I got a call from a friend on the L.A. City Council, the group that really controlled the DWP, saying that I needed their approval. I feigned ignorance, and they then ratified what I had underway. I handled the DWP Board somewhat gingerly since I did need their approval for anything important. The L.A. City Council, which was liberal, had my back, as they hated the conservative Mayor and his appointees. I was kind of fireproof, and I took full advantage of the tension between the City Council and the Mayor.

We reduced our cost of electricity by reducing the payroll. I then froze the electric rates for years to come and had sufficient cash flow to dramatically reduce the DWP generating plant debt from $7 billion to $3 billion in four short years. Having established my reputation as a tough cost cutter, I was then able to launch energy efficiency and solar energy programs without much opposition from a conservative Mayor Riordan and a conservative Board of Directors.

The DWP made renewable energy, or green power, a reality in 1998 with a program that offered it to customers who were willing to pay a bit more (three cents per kilowatt-hour) for their electricity. We put solar power on the roofs of municipal buildings, such as the LA Convention Center. We also made energy efficiency a reality with our just-do-it program, which was so popular we didn't dare advertise it. The DWP efficiency experts went to low-income neighborhoods and just did stuff on the job, like caulking holes in buildings, cleaning refrigerator coils, replacing broken windows, and installing efficient light bulbs and showerheads without charging anyone any money. A typical visit cut folks' electric bill by 20 percent.

Rick Caruso, a very wealthy and successful developer, was the Chair of the DWP Board. We hardly agreed on anything. Rick was very smart, and he did respect my success in cutting costs. He also understood that the City Council backed me, and he needed their approval of his shopping center projects. He soon learned he couldn't order me to do things just because he said so.

Once in a closed session, just after I had succeeded in reducing the payroll by one thousand people, Mr. Caruso, who was very anti-union, said, "Dave, don't hire any replacements." I shot back that I'd hire them if I needed them, unless he placed a hiring freeze on the public Board agenda, got it approved, and not vetoed, by the City Council. That ended the conversation. After that, Board President Caruso and I understood each other, and we got along just fine.

The real glory days for my leadership at the DWP came when the lights stayed on in LA while the rest of California suffered blackouts under deregulation. The California Public Utilities Commission had required investor-owned regulated utilities to sell their generating plants, and they did not have long-term contracts for their own supply. They were at the mercy of the generating companies, such as Enron, a Texas energy company, and other such companies that owned the power plants. The generating companies created artificial power shortages and runaway prices for electricity throughout the State of California, but not in LA, where the DWP still owned its own generating plants.

When I became general manager, the DWP board had already approved a proposal to turn over the DWP's power plants to a private company. I helped kill that proposal; as a result, when the shortages occurred in the rest of the state, the LADWP still had plenty of power, even a surplus to sell to the state to help them avoid even worse blackouts. It doesn't get much better than when you are able to keep the lights on, especially at Christmas. The rates stayed flat in Los Angeles while the rest of the state experienced blackouts and large rate increases.

Those were the days that the DWP was the toast of the town and I came close to being considered a hero. We made front-page positive news in the *LA Times*, and I was able to advance my green power and energy efficiency programs without opposition from a conservative DWP board and LA mayor. The DWP earned more than $200 million selling surplus power to the state during the crisis. We accepted the price the state offered for our power. All the money, of course, went to benefit LA ratepayers. But that didn't stop folks from calling me a *bandit* a year later, when my appointment to a state position went before the state legislature for confirmation.

The truth was that the DWP and the other California utilities went to great lengths to help the state. One evening when the state faced a massive blackout, at the urgent request of the state, I joined with John Bryson, CEO of Southern California Edison, to purchase power for the state in the Pacific Northwest. We delivered the power over the transmission lines we owned. To make matters worse, the state didn't even pay us; they charged it. I had no authority to do this, and I am not sure the city of LA ever forgave me, but we did get paid seven years later.

The LADWP general manager doesn't often get to meet even a former head of state of another country, but I had that privilege. I hosted Mikhail Gorbachev, the president of the former Soviet Union. He attended a symposium on water quality that the LADWP sponsored. I took him on a tour of LA in the DWP helicopter. He looked down and saw all the big homes with private swimming pools. He said to me, "This is the first time that I realized just how rich the United States really is."

A year later, he was in California again to speak at a big-shot conference in Bakersfield. His interpreter called me to ask if I would fly him from LA to Bakersfield in our helicopter, saying that Mr. Gorbachev thought it was "demeaning for the former head of the Soviet Union to arrive in a car like an ordinary citizen." I was glad to oblige and had another opportunity to get to know him better. He told me he felt strongly that he had volunteered to end the Cold War for the benefit of the Russian people, not for fear of the United States. He also refused to talk about the nuclear disaster on his watch at Chernobyl. He did say he favored developing wind power in Crimea. He was very friendly and easy to converse with.

SETTLING AN EIGHTY-FIVE-YEAR WATER WAR

Water was as big of an issue as electric power at the Department of Water and Power. My biggest water accomplishment was making peace with the people in the Owens Valley, where much of LA's water supply originates. When I first became general manager, LA faced an order from the Great Basin Air Quality District (GBAQD) in that region, requiring the LADWP to control the dust and do so at once. People from the mayor's office and city council staff members were negotiating with the GBAQD, trying to settle the dispute over having drained it. The LA negotiating team wasn't very anxious to settle the dispute and was really looking for a fight in court, even though the law was very much in favor of the GBAQD. I took over the negotiations in the spring of 1998. We reached an agreement by the fall of that year.

The big problem on both sides was lack of trust. This feud had gone on for eighty-five years. The Owens Valley people thought we took their water without adequate compensation and left them with a dry lake. The people at city hall felt that the dust from the dry lake wasn't all that bad, that there were just a few people up there, that nothing would grow anyhow, and that fixing the dry lake wasn't worth all the money it would cost to control the dust.

LA was afraid that the answer would be to put water back into the lake. The water from the Owens Lake is a main supply of water in a region—the LA area—that is essentially a desert. On days with high winds, which happen quite a few times a year, the dust became so thick that it looked like a storm. People who lived there represented by the GBAQD thought that was a hazard to their health and were determined to get it controlled. Federal authorities at the EPA considered it the biggest air particulate—or dust pollution—problem in the entire United States. The DWP was clearly in violation of the air quality laws.

My toughest bargaining was with the LA city council staff, which preferred to litigate rather than settle. By comparison, the air quality folks in the Owens Valley were actually easy to deal with. In a few short months, we worked out a compromise. They agreed to give us at least six years to stop the dust pollution, a time to perfect nonwater methods to control the dust, and the LADWP agreed to meet the federal air quality standards. We consummated the agreement in the fall of 1998 by getting it through the city council machinery, which was the toughest part. It was implemented, and LA enjoyed good relations with the Owens Valley for the first time in eighty-five years.

Another water-related problem we solved was over the filtration plants the DWP needed to build at DWP reservoirs in Encino and the northern San Fernando Valley in the LA suburbs. Open reservoirs to store water needed to comply with stringent quality standards. Because the water coming into these reservoirs sat in the reservoirs and collected algae and minute contaminants from the air, it needed to be continuously filtered. Fairly expensive homes surrounded each of the reservoirs. The residents were upset about the big construction projects that were needed to build the large, ugly filtration plants, a typical don't-disturb-my-nest reaction. But my problem was each plant would cost more than $100 million.

I took a fresh look at the matter, asking whether we really needed these reservoirs in the twenty-first century. The DWP had more than enough sources of water coming into LA to meet residents' present and future needs and to keep up the water pressure—including the connection to the Metropolitan Water District, a huge supplier of water. We decided to keep the reservoirs full as a standby source of water in case of an unforeseen emergency, but not to use the water on a daily basis. This enabled us to install very small filtration plants that were much less expensive and weren't eyesores. Here again, a solution motivated by environmental and aesthetic considerations ended up saving a significant amount of public money—about $100 million.

California's Governor Davis was in serious political trouble in the year 2000 because of the blackouts caused by generating company manipulators who created an artificial shortage of reasonably priced electricity in the state. I had become a sort-of hero, as LA avoided the blackouts and rate increases, so in early 2001, Governor Davis asked me to take a leave from the DWP and help him put an end to the crisis. With Mayor Riordan's approval, I joined a troubleshooting team headed by Mike Peevey, a friend who later chaired the CPUC, which included Vikram Budhraja.

Vikram and I negotiated a number of long-term contracts with generating companies at reasonable prices. In addition, we suggested a mind-blowing idea to conserve energy that Governor Davis adopted. We offered a 20 percent bonus for customers, which cut their usage by 20 percent. One-third of customers took just that in the summer of 2001, and this reduced demand enough to avoid any further blackouts.

We asked the electric-generating companies to meet with us one at a time and hammered out deals with about six of them. The contracts were valuable, since they provided the basis for financing the construction of new power plants that avoided future power shortages. But we insisted, as part of the long-term deal, on getting some reasonably priced power right away to help end the crisis, and we were successful.

Even so, we caught hell from lots of folks at the time. Senator Burton, the Democrat leader of the state senate, proclaimed that we had "bought too much power at too high a price for too long a term." I took some pride in later years in learning that Calpine, the company that agreed to our first contract, claimed that the price was so low it was driving them into bankruptcy. The combination of contracting for large amounts of reasonably priced power and customers conserving did indeed bring an early end to the crisis by the summer of 2001. Even so, it was too late to save Governor Davis's job. He was voted out in a special election a year later.

I returned to my job at the DWP in March 2001 and continued my focus on energy efficiency and renewable energy. I also began a serious effort to reduce the amount of highly polluting coal that was the source of most of the DWP's electricity. We sold our interests in a coal plant in Montana and our interests in the Mojave coal plant in the Four Corners area. In fact, our efforts ultimately led to the complete closure of the Mojave power plant, which was polluting the air over the Grand Canyon and endangering the health and homes of members of the Navajo tribe.

Friendship and work seemed to be my pattern in those days, as I gained another long-term friend when Kim Mizrahi and I met. She lobbied me on behalf of the Navajo Nation that lived near the coal mining for the Mojave power plant, claiming it was ruining the lives of the Navajo. She persuaded me to visit the strip-mining and the plant itself to see for myself. That visit persuaded me to sell the DWP's share of Mojave and then try to get the plant closed.

Kim became my environmental conscience. She moved to France and lived in a solar-powered yurt. Our active friendship included many wonderful trips together over the years. We lived in different worlds and learned from each other and had lots of fun in the process. Our friendship continued for eighteen years and then came to an abrupt end in 2015. I did learn that a friendship with a woman can be as heartwarming as a love affair.

A meeting with consumer activists in LA resulted in another lifelong friendship. Ralph Nader was my guest at the LADWP, and his presence attracted a sizable crowd for a sit-down discussion. That crowd included Kim but also Susan Cox, who was advancing green power by teaching kids in school about the horror of fossil fuels and the joy of solar power. We called her the *green-power girl*, and she, too, became a friend—a friendship that continues as of my ninetieth year. Susan helped me in my next adventure, running for elected office, but I digress.

My success in keeping the lights on in LA while much of California was blacked out went to my head. I guess I felt I could do mostly anything, so I decided to run for the California State Assembly in 2001 while I was still the general manager at the DWP. I did take a leave of absence in the last weeks of the campaign.

I raised four hundred thousand dollars in campaign contributions from friends and wealthy folks who thought I would win. I am ashamed to admit that I took money from folks like Ken Lay of Enron fame, who disagreed with my beliefs. He did not change my views at all, but still, I saw how easy it was to look past one's principles when it came to raising money for public office. I did it even though I hated doing it.

I sent out lots of mail. We even wrote a booklet about me and mailed it out. But I didn't have much of a ground campaign. I loved to make speeches but hated to knock on people's doors. It turned out I didn't really like campaigning. I was just bored with the DWP after all the excitement of working for Governor Davis during the energy crisis.

I came in second to Fran Pavley, who turned out to be a fine legislator. The people who voted were correct—she was the better candidate. I did have a good concession speech: "I love Fran, and Fran loves me. She sent me back to the DWP." My defeat really didn't shake my self-confidence. In retrospect, I was more interested in running for office than serving.

In 2001, the city attorney James Hahn was running for mayor. As part of his campaign, he sent me a letter on city attorney stationery, blasting the DWP for proposing an unpopular water-recycling project. What I proposed was recycling wastewater in a process that made it completely clean and reusable, rather than just dumping it into the ocean. Opponents called this recycling *toilet to tap* and killed it. In view of the drought in California in later years, I was clearly on the right track but way too early. City Attorney Hahn, catering to public opinion, gave his letter to the press before it was delivered to me. The city attorney was the DWP's lawyer. I told the press that if Hahn were in private law practice, I would have fired him. "What he did was unethical." It made the news.

Obviously, I was not worried about keeping my job if he became mayor because I sure had burned my bridge with James Hahn, who did get elected. But without any thought about the impact of my outspoken blast at Hahn, I automatically made a friend in his opponent, Antonio Villaraigosa, who became the mayor in 2005.

The California energy crisis was still in full swing in 2001 even though there were no blackouts. The DWP was in good shape, but I had just about worn out my welcome with Republican Mayor Riordan, his successor James Hahn, and the business-friendly DWP board, who were not in favor of my green initiatives. I actually was planning to accept an offer from San Francisco mayor Willie Brown to head a smaller public utility in San Francisco when I received another offer from Governor Davis. He asked me to return to Sacramento in late 2001 to head the newly created California Consumer Power Authority (CCPA). I told Mayor Brown about the offer, and he said, "Grey needs you more than I do." I resigned from the DWP and took the job the governor offered me.

The CCPA was part of the package of laws enacted in response to the energy crisis. Our job was to see that enough power plants were built even if private utilities didn't build them. Unfortunately, we were a "paper tiger" because we had no authority to borrow money or purchase power, and we really had no serious funding. We were marginally useful in creating a close working relationship among various California energy agencies, and we tried hard to get a lot of peaking power plants built to avoid shortages but were not very successful.

The most lasting memory of my failed tenure as president of the CCPA was the confirmation hearing on my appointment before the California State Senate. The debate lasted for hours, one of the longest in state history. All the Republicans were opposed to me as the symbol of the energy crisis, for which they blamed Governor Davis. I needed every Democrat vote to be confirmed, and many of them were skeptical.

The main problem the Democrats had with me was envy of my role as manager of the LADWP, which earned $200 million in profits selling surplus power to the state. One senator called me a "public power Ken Lay [the head of Enron, the chief Texas manipulator]." I replied there was a big difference: "I didn't make a red cent—the money all went to the LA customers." Senator Piece from San Diego was first opposed to me until I reminded him that as GM, I had tried to sell surplus power directly to San Diego at a low price, but the LA mayor had stopped me. I also explained that LA had sold $100 million of power to the state on credit and they had not paid us yet. I got his vote.

It finally came down to the vote of a Democratic senator who had made investigating the crisis his career. He was going to vote against me until Richie Ross, his campaign manager (who had managed my failed campaign), told him that killing my nomination was a sure way for him to piss off more good people than he could ever count. He made a speech blasting me but voted for my confirmation—the vote that saved the day. After the vote, I thanked Senator Piece, and he said, "Dave, I could have made just as good a speech against you." It was a close call.

The most lasting success of the CCPA was my recruitment of Laura Doll from Texas as my deputy. She remained in California and has been a significant player at the CPUC and elsewhere. She has also become a lifelong personal friend I cherish.

BACK TO LA

I called it quits at the CCPA in 2003 and returned to Los Angeles, where I formed a partnership with Ari Swiller and Cole Frates in an outfit we called the Renewable Resources Group, which continues to be very successful to this day. Our first major venture at the Renewable Resources Group was to create a hydrogen car company. The Ford Motor Company engineers assured us that it would only require a small amount of tinkering for a standard internal combustion auto engine to burn hydrogen. Furthermore, hydrogen fuel tanks were commercially available and safe.

The Ford engineers were correct but were never able to get Ford management, or any other manufacturer, interested in a hydrogen-burning combustion engine car. A main reason was there were no hydrogen filling stations. California governor Arnold Schwarzenegger, who succeeded Governor Davis in 2003, proposed a hydrogen highway but never came up with public or private funding to build it.

The beauty of hydrogen is that when you burn it, even in an ordinary internal combustion engine, you only emit water vapor, no pollutants. But the idea of burning hydrogen in an internal combustion auto engine really never got rolling. Hydrogen is usually associated with the fuel cell, which converts hydrogen into electricity and is vastly more efficient than the internal combustion engine. The fuel-cell car has long been a dream of the auto industry, and it is finally beginning to come true. In fact, fuel-cell electric cars, along with all-electric cars, are certainly the cars of the future. Survival of life on this planet, as we now know it, depends on the speed with which renewable electricity and renewable hydrogen replace fossil fuels and nuclear power.

Our Renewable Resources Group acquired other clients, but we did make an effort with the hydrogen car before we gave up. At one point, we had famous car designer Carroll Shelby's "hot car" running on hydrogen. We also attempted to set up a business in Iceland, where hydrogen cars would have been cheaper than gasoline cars because of the 100 percent tariff on gasoline-powered cars. But we couldn't find anyone in Iceland to perform the business promotion that we needed.

I enjoyed working with my partners Ari Swiller and Cole Frates. Our business, though not exciting compared to public service, went well. We were pioneers in advancing renewable energy. Ari and Cole remain friends, but by 2005, I was anxious to get back into public service. That opportunity came along with the election of Antonio Villaraigosa as mayor of Los Angeles. I was a friend of Antonio's, and I helped raise money and support for him during his campaign. I silently had hoped he would name me the head of the board of directors of the Los Angeles Department of Water and Power, which I formerly managed. But after the election, he told me that position had already been promised to Mary Nichols. Instead, the mayor named me to chair the board overseeing of the Port of Los Angeles even though my prior experience with the shipping industry had happened more than sixty years before as a merchant seaman.

The main problem at the Port of Los Angeles was air pollution, and I had earned a reputation at TVA and elsewhere as a clean air champion. I also had a lot of experience at the DWP in earlier years in how to effect change in the LA city government. Mayor Villaraigosa proclaimed a policy of green growth for the port and named four other like-minded commissioners and a new energetic general manager named Geraldine Knatz to work with me as president of the board.

The LA Port job turned out to be one of the most successful gigs of my life. The port's traffic had grown rapidly for years, and the level of air pollution had grown just as fast or faster. The people of San Pedro and Wilmington, California, lived literally at the doorstep of the Port of Los Angeles and were suffering from the air pollution caused by the big ships at the dock and the dirty trucks that hauled the cargo away.

The Natural Resources Defense Council and other local environmental groups had unsuccessfully been trying to get the port to clean up. The former mayor James Hahn and environmentalists had settled on a no-net-increase policy, which meant reducing pollution down to the levels in 2001. I read their report, which stated that at the 2001 level, the premature deaths of 3,500 people a year would be cut in half to 1,750 people. My reaction at a public meeting was I could not believe we should have a goal of killing 1,750 people a year. It was a deliberately shocking statement designed to tell the folks we were serious about cleaning the air. I then stated that we had to meet air quality standards and stop the killing. This was such a dramatic change from the past that we quickly won the support of the local communities, the Natural Resources Defense Council, and other activists, which was extremely helpful, indeed essential, to pursuing our green growth policies.

What we said to the shipping industry, terminal operators, trucking companies, and railroads was that we would only approve expansions they needed if they resulted in cleanup measures that actually resulted in rapid reductions in the existing level of pollution. The goal was to attain legally approved clean air in a few short years. For the ships, we made them agree on as rapid a timetable as possible to power their ships at the docks with electricity, and in the interim, we provided incentives for using cleaner fuel to power their ships near or at our docks. For the trucks, we adopted a clean truck program with an early timetable of dates when dirty trucks would no longer be allowed at the port—only new trucks that met stringent air quality standards. In addition, we, along with the South Coast Air Quality Management District, funded research that developed a commercially viable all-electric truck for short-haul traffic. Of most significance is the fact that in the four-year period from 2005 to 2009, we actually implemented these programs and reduced local air pollution by 70 percent.

President of the LA Port is not a paid job, and ordinarily, that person merely presides over monthly public meetings of the board he or she chairs. I was much more directly involved working with the staff, and I spent much of my time shaping and implementing the new green growth policies we adopted. I had a very close and good working relationship with our new General Manager Geraldine Knatz.

A key factor in our success was my early public statements followed by policy action that persuaded the local activists that they finally had port management on their side fighting for cleaner air. The fact that the American Trucking Associations sued the port to block our program created an enemy. The port joined with local activists, environmental organizations, and labor unions to oppose the *mother truckers*, as we called them in private.

A great fear we had was that the truckers—who opposed our clean-up-or-don't-come approach—would simply not come and would stop the enormous flow of traffic through our port. The fear was very real as our deadlines for no more dirty trucks approached. The large trucking companies had not been serving the port, and despite our financial help, the little guys could well decide not to buy clean trucks. So early one morning, a key staff person and I flew to Phoenix, Arizona, for a private meeting with the Swift Trucking Company, a large outfit that owned lots of clean trucks but was not serving the Port of LA. Luckily, the CEO of Swift was a former truck driver who had served LA, and he took great pride—and a serious business risk—in agreeing that his company would handle the business if others didn't show.

This was the kind of initiative by a board president that was new to the port—yes, it violated all my rules about micromanaging, but I did it because I felt it was necessary and the manager was okay with my active role.

A major element of our success in pollution control at the Port of LA was doing it jointly with our sister Port of Long Beach. We were next door to each other, and unless we both cleaned up, the air would still be dirty. I reached out to the president of the Long Beach Port when I first took office, and we held the first joint public meeting in the long history of the two port boards. I remember it clearly because in public, I mispronounced the name of Mayor Villaraigosa, who honored us with his presence. He made a hand motion of cutting off my head. But the meeting was the beginning of a beautiful friendship between the two ports, which succeeded in reducing pollution over the entire San Pedro Bay airshed, even though the partnership did fall out over a number of other issues years later.

Another key element of our success was that we had a united board of commissions. As president, chairing the public meetings, I adopted the policy that if one commissioner had a problem with an agenda item, we all had a problem; then we talked it out and reached an agreement. As a result, all our decisions over a four-year period were unanimous. I had finally figured out how to handle people—you need to listen to them.

I chaired the port board meetings with a lively sense of humor. I know that is a braggy, self-serving statement, but it is true. In fact, our general manager collected a list of my one-liners. An example is when someone appearing before the board, which had a three-minute limit on speakers, asked, "Mr. Freeman, how much time do I have left?" I answered, "That's up to the Lord, but here, you've only got thirty seconds." Another one that the mayor pretended to love was my public comment that I was more concerned about meeting my maker than my mayor.

During my Port of LA years, I continued my lifelong interest in the study of energy and the environment. I felt it was time for the renewable revolution to begin and replace both nuclear and fossil fuels. I did research and wrote a book, published in 2007, that explained how we could do without the "three poisons"—nuclear, coal, and oil. I must admit that I didn't realize then that as an emitter of greenhouse gases, natural gas is a poison of equal magnitude.

I was riding high by 2009, with our work at the port being cited as a model of success. My life pattern shows that success always leads to another challenge; Mayor Villaraigosa gave it to me in the spring of 2009, when he asked me to leave the port and become his deputy for energy and environment for a job well done. That job included overseeing the DWP as well as the port, working directly for the mayor, who had just been reelected for another four years.

I was instrumental in persuading the mayor to adopt a very green agenda for the DWP in his second inaugural message in July 2009. In that message, he directed the DWP to have contracts in place before he left office in 2013 for getting off coal by 2020. He also directed the DWP to achieve 40 percent renewables by 2020. And he ordered a number of green initiatives for the DWP's power and water operations.

The first major problem I encountered was that the general manager at the DWP was at war with his entire top staff and the very influential union leader Brian D'Arcy. I orchestrated a solution in which the general manager decided to resign and that brought some temporary peace to that situation. But a leaderless DWP was not a solution to anything. The mayor decided that I should take over as acting general manager in October 2009 while we recruited a permanent manager who would carry out our aggressive green agenda.

An early issue was the DWP's struggle to build a high-voltage overhead transmission line called the Green Line from Southern California to LA. The five routes considered through pristine desert lands angered thousands of folks who lived near the proposed paths. They now had a common enemy in the DWP. I studied the issues and decided the DWP did not need the new transmission line. I canceled the project, and that, of course, stopped the opposition. Since the project was the brainchild of the former general manager hated by staff, it was a popular move internally as well.

As acting general manager, I decided the DWP really needed an increase in rates if it were going to have the funds we needed to go green or even to operate the utility reliably. I did institute major cuts in the budget, but they were not sufficient to avoid a rate increase. The city council wisely hired an independent consultant to examine whether our rate increase was justified. The council's consultant's report suggested we needed an even greater rate increase than what we requested. The city council ignored its own consultant's report, but we still felt confident in our lobbying effort. We thought we were gaining council confidence that a rate increase was needed. Then, as 2009 came to a close, stuff really hit the fan.

I was acting GM on leave from my position as deputy mayor, frankly without a mandate to make any major changes. But I was the mayor's guy, and the DWP was making progress on our green agenda. Then without informing me, the Mayor named Austin Beutner, an LA billionaire, his deputy mayor and agreed that Austin would be in charge of the DWP and the Port. That left me in the awkward position of being acting GM and reporting to someone who had been given my permanent responsibilities in the mayor's office. In other words, I had no authority, and everyone in the DWP and the council knew it.

But Austin chose not to get his hands dirty in the fight with city council to raise the electric rates, and he and the mayor authorized one of Austin's deputies, Jim Carson, to manage the rate increase campaign. Jim ordered me not to speak with anyone on the city council and proceeded to enlarge the request for a rate increase to include a large additional sum he argued to put in a lockbox. This sum was to be used only for additional renewable energy projects to meet our 40 percent goal by 2020. I obviously was excited about this support for renewables but felt that it was politically stupid and would endanger our getting any rate increase at all. Along with the DWP board president, we told Carson and all the top staff people in a private meeting that the added increase was crazy. But Carson pursued that option anyhow.

The rate increase decision came to a head in March 2010 while I was in Israel with my family for the bar mitzvah celebration of one of my nephew's sons. While in Israel, I received the most awful phone call of my life from a professional point of view. The mayor's chief of staff, Jeff Carr, called me to say Mayor Villaraigosa had directed him to call me in Israel and tell me that he decided to name Austin Beutner acting general manager of the DWP when my six-month term ended in April. Jeff stated that the mayor said he was under pressure from the business community to replace me because of the rate increase. I asked if the mayor had anything else to say to me, and the chief of staff said no. He then added that this was the most difficult phone call he ever had to make, and he made it "only at the of the mayor."

I returned from Israel after the rate increase debacle that occurred while I was away. The city council was extremely angry because the mayor rejected an increase the council approved that wasn't quite as large as what the mayor requested. The City Council accused the DWP of blackmail, claiming DWP withheld i payments owed the City unless the Council approved their rate increase. These two items were connected because the city charter required that the DWP declare a surplus before it could make payments to the city's general fund. Without the rate increase, the DWP had a deficit, not a surplus. So it wasn't blackmail, but the City Council, angry over the Mayor's rejection of the increases they approved, chose to call it that.

My term as acting general manager of the DWP ended in April 2010. Since the mayor had given my prior responsibilities as his deputy to Mr. Beutner, I left city government. In truth, I was effectively fired. The mayor made no public statement about my departure.

I did have a final good-bye meeting with Mayor Villaraigosa, which his chief of staff, Jeff Carr, also attended. Unbelievably, Mayor Villaraigosa looked me directly in the eyes and said, "Dave, you have got to reassure me that you recognize that I have always been loyal to you." I couldn't believe his words and didn't have the heart, or the courage, to tell him that he was wrong. He really believed he was loyal to me, and while I worked for him, that was true, but emotionally, he could not accept responsibility for his own acts. But Antonio did give me four years of public service at the Port, for which I am grateful, and he does still remain my friend.

Later, just before I moved from LA to DC, my friend Mike Peevey, then president of the CPUC, hosted a good-bye party for me. There, in front of a couple hundred people (no reporters), Mayor Villaraigosa stated that I was the most loyal person he knew and that I had tried to sell his ideas to the city council even when I opposed them. On that bizarre note, my tenure in the Villaraigosa administration ended, at the age of eighty-four.

RETIREMENT: A FRIEND OF THE EARTH

I took full advantage of my newfound freedom. My best male friend, Robert Floyd, and I and his son Jason took off on August 20, 2010, for a trip around the world. The itinerary included Seoul, South Korea; Saint Petersburg, Russia; Prague, Czech Republic; and Paris, France. The lasting impression Korea left on me was that Seoul was a well-planned city where traffic flowed much more smoothly than in LA. The Koreans were thin and healthy, and the militarized zone on the boundary with North Korea reminded me of Disneyland. The pride the people of Saint Petersburg had in their city left another lasting memory, not to mention their museums and golden domes.

The trip around the world excited my interest in travel, so trips to Israel, Japan, elsewhere in France, Germany, Switzerland, Cuba, Bolivia, and Mexico followed. I was fortunate enough to get better acquainted with a beautiful artist named Liz Marx in Los Angeles. She and I have enjoyed some beautiful journeys together over the years. Unfortunately for me, I only got to really know her as I was planning to move away from Los Angeles. But our warm friendship and travels together have continued despite the fact we live three thousand miles apart.

Life out of public office in Los Angeles left me with an empty feeling. In early 2011, I made the decision to move to the District of Columbia, where I would be in direct contact with two of my three children and seven out of nine grandchildren, and now one great-grandchild! I repaired my condo and, with the help of my friend Kim Mizrahi from France, cleaned out and threw away a ton of stuff. Moving is a very cleansing act. I actually moved to DC in May 2011.

Shortly after arriving in DC in 2011, I met Damon Moglen, who headed the energy and climate work for Friends of the Earth. It led to a new adventure the likes of which I did not visualize when we first met. Damon and I hit it off immediately and decided it was time for Friends of the Earth to take the lead in a public campaign to end nuclear power in California. The reason was that the two nuclear plants in California were both near earthquake faults, more than thirty years old, and right on the Pacific Ocean, where they were subject to tsunami waves. They were in danger of causing a Fukushima-type disaster in California.

We first thought to put an initiative on the California presidential ballot in November 2012. FOE wisely did some polling and found that even after Fukushima, the people of California did not fear the two existing nuclear plants. In fact, they were more in fear of the radioactive waste that had piled up for thirty years at each plant's site. We concluded that we did not have the time or resources to fully inform the public and offset the billion-dollar-or-more campaign of opposition that the Southern California Edison Company and Pacific Gas and Electric would undoubtedly fund against the proposition. We then decided we would launch an educational campaign with the hopes that it would turn into a ballot measure a year later.

Then, in January 2012, San Onofre had a radioactive leak from a defective steam generator, and the plant was shut down for repairs. It was like a canary in a coal mine, speaking to us and saying, "Shut me down for good before I kill you." Our campaign then focused like a laser beam on San Onofre. Wisely, our first move was to find out the facts about why there was a leak from the steam generator in Unit 2 and why the Edison Company also kept Unit 3 shut down. The crucial event was that FOE obtained significant funding from an unnamed donor who lived in the danger zone near the San Onofre plant.

In the early months of the campaign, Friends of the Earth contracted for and published reports by Arnie Gundersen, an independent nuclear engineer, explaining exactly what was wrong with the steam generators at San Onofre. To cut to the chase, we found that the design had a significant mistake that resulted in the leak in the steam generators; the defect was inherent in the design, and these steam generators were beyond repair. The Edison Company was still in public denial and laid out plans to reopen both units.

We then developed a strategy that consisted of the following two actions: (1) legal action at the Nuclear Regulatory Commission (NRC) to prevent, or at least delay, the restart of the plant and (2) legal action at the California Public Utilities Commission to force Edison's shareholders to pay for their disregard for safety and, more important, show that restarting the plant safely was not economical.

In addition to the cost to replace the steam generators, we showed it would cost billions of dollars to install cooling towers to comply with the state policy of stopping the giant fish kills from sucking in huge volumes of ocean water to absorb the waste heat from the reactors. Another major future cost was to rebuild the plant to withstand earthquakes. The campaign also included recruiting local activists, issuing press releases and TV spots to excite local public opposition to reopening the plant.

To carry out the strategy, we filed a petition with the NRC, which resulted in three separate actions, all demanding we be given a chance to present our evidence to NRC judges before Edison was allowed to restart the plant. We also persuaded the CPUC to launch an investigation to discover who was at fault and who was to pay for all the extra costs caused by the plant shutdown. We obtained local support for our campaign from mayors and councilmembers in Southern California, Senator Boxer, and Congressman Markey, a leading nuclear opponent from Massachusetts.

We designed the strategy to persuade the Edison Company that closing the plant was a better financial bet than continuing the fight. We gained a victory at the NRC when a three-judge tribunal ruled in our favor, raising a serious question of how long the plant would remain shut. Also, the CPUC made it clear that if the proof showed that Edison did ignore safety concerns, their shareholders would take a beating. But the fight was still on.

A critical breakthrough occurred when FOE obtained access to letters Edison had withheld from our discovery process at the CPUC. The smoking gun was a 2004 letter from an Edison vice president that revealed Edison knew it was taking a safety risk by going ahead with constructing the steam generators without fixing the safety concern in their design. He predicted a disaster if they didn't fix the safety concern, which they did not do. We made that letter available to the staff of Mr. Peevey, the CPUC president. Shortly thereafter, in June 2013, Edison announced it was closing the plant permanently. We finally got the *New York Times* to write about San Onofre on that date, on which they reported, "San Onofre is dead."

I must say, this last "job" as an unpaid advisor and activist with FOE gave me a different and indeed more egocentric sense of achievement than public service. The David-versus-Goliath nature of the fight did it.

But the fight goes on. Diablo Canyon is the remaining nuclear plant in California—sitting very near four earthquake faults.

Diablo Canyon, located near Saint Louis Ibisco on the Pacific Ocean in Northern California. That plant is located near sizable earthquake faults all discovered after the plant was under construction in the late 1970's. No one would even consider locating a nuclear plant at that location today. Even so, in 2013 we found that the utility owner, PG&E, had already applied to the NRC for a 20-year license extension so that the giant 2 unit plant would continue to operate until 2045!

I continued to spend most of my "working" hours in my role as Senior Advisor at F.O.E. We decided we could not "quit winners" after the San Onofre victory but rather must launch a strategic campaign to prevent Death Canyon from obtaining that 20- year license extension.

We learned from the San Onofre campaign that the sudden shutdown of a large nuclear plant resulted in its replacement by natural gas powered electricity with a resulting spike in the emission of greenhouse gases. We therefore decided that our campaign for Diablo Canyon was not just to shut it down but rather to achieve an orderly replacement with a portfolio made up of energy efficiency, renewable energy, and storage capacity. The campaign thus addressed both the both the dangers of nuclear power and climate change, the two greatest threats facing mankind.

F.O.E. had limited financial resources for the campaign so that the staff consisted of just my dear friend Damon Moglen and me, as an unpaid volunteer.

Our strategy was to "persuade" the PG&E management that operating the plant beyond its existing license was uneconomical and posed too many obstacles for the utility to want to take on. We knew that protests wouldn't be persuasive. We needed a strategy that combined the force of law and making the plant so expensive that renewable energy would actually be lower in cost.

We launched a 4 pronged attack,

(1) At the Federal Nuclear Regulatory Commission we filed a petition challenging the safety of the plan claiming that the earthquake threat was stronger than what the plant was designed to withstand.
(2) At the California Public Utilities Commission we filed a petition claiming that operating the plant beyond its licence was uneconomical, that a combination of energy efficiency, renewables and storage was lower in cost.
(3) At the California Water Reserves Board we claimed that PG&E needed to build cooling towers that would cost between 2-8 billion dollars to comply with their policy of stopping the massive fish kill caused by using the ocean water to remove the waste heat from the power plant. If

the cooling towers were ordered this cost alone would render the plant uneconomic.

(4) AT the California State Lands Commission we discovered that PG&E's lease for Diablo's cooling water intake structure expired in 2018. They were seeking a new lease from 2018 to 2024-5, assuming that it could be obtained without controversy since it was just for the time to match its existing NRC licence and did not, in their view, raise the issue of license extension. F.O.E opposed the license extension claiming an environmental review was required before it could be approved. And State Lands appeared receptive to our view.

In the press we called attention to the danger from earthquakes that could be stronger than the plant could withstand and achieved some front-page coverage in the California press.

The campaign gathered steam slowly and by 2015 PG&E was stating publicly that they were still considering whether to seek license extension for the 2025 to 2045 period. The prospect of facing a multi-billion dollar investment in cooling towers and the, uncertainty of whether State Lands would grant them an extended license on reasonable terms, undoubtedly caused them to pause and reconsider.

F.O.E. funded an expert study that we called "Plan B". It proved in great detail that the nuclear plant could be economically replaced by a portfolio of energy efficiency, a renewable resources and storage. Rather than publishing the report we invited PG&E to review it. This lead to a meeting at which F.O.E. and PG&E agreed to try to reach an agreement.

F.O.E invited the Natural Resource Defense Council to join in the negotiations which finally culminated in an agreement announced on June 21, 2016.

Under this agreement the nuclear plant will cease operation in 2024-25 and be replaced by a portfolio of greenhouse gas-free resources as F.O.E. advocated.

With this agreement California's electric power will become nuclear-free and a giant step forward 100% renewables will be taken.

In addition to my work with F.O.E. I wrote another book entitled "All-Electric America". Leah Parks was my co-author. It suggests a course of action for America to follow that would contain the dangers of both nuclear power and climate change. It is by no means a bestseller but stay tuned.

PERSONAL LIFE SURPRISES

My personal life back in Washington, DC from 2011 to 2016 had its own events worthy of note.

It's a pretty good idea to get to know your family while you are still alive. I was lucky to get to do so. My son Roger shares my environmental interests and also his "love life." thus I bonded with him even though he lives in Denver. But with Anita and Stan, my other two children, I really became family since they live in the D.C. area.

I have learned to admire Anita's devotion to her teaching career with children that have speech and hearing problems. She works harder, for less pay, than my sons. She is the most genuinely helpful person I know – constantly finding ways to help everyone in her life.

Getting a first-hand view of Stan's accomplishments as a very prominent lawyer has been a joy to behold. His interests are far more varied than mine and he has financed all five of his kids attendance at Ivy league colleges. His financial and professional success has not changed his low-key, friendly personality.

Roger is not in D.C. but he is so fully engaged in life that his presence is always felt. He has been the dominant parent that raised two wonderful young ladies. He is undergoing a number of challenges at the moment but I am confident he will soon become a full-time environmental activist making use of his extraordinary legal talent and desire to make the world a better place.

And there are the grandkids, the young ladies, LIsa, Karen, Tess, Kelsey and Carolyn-and the young men Nate, Alex. Ben and Tim. All 9 of them are precious to me. They are all employed or still in college. It is a joy to watch them become successful adults – and they are all quite successful.

And now there is Charles – my great grandson, a young man that has made me "great"!

My second life in D.C. has focused on family and with Damon Moglen at F.O.E. who has become family. But I have continued to travel and I am lucky to have friends, most of whom are female. Unfortunately most of my male friends have passed away.

One of my 40-year long friends is Mary Aubry. She lives in the same apartment building as me. Mary and I have a complicated history but we are now at peace with each other and enjoy hanging out together fairly often.

I still enjoy seeing other lifelong friends in California– Angelina Galiteva and her two kids– Isabella and Nicholas are like family to me. And Susan Cox will always be in my life as a wonderful reminder that brains and beauty can come together. I met Liz Marx just as I left L.A. yet our friendship has continued to grow. But some things do change, and in the most unexpected way.

One friendship that I thought was eternal was with Kim Mizrahi who was my beautiful environmental conscience that lived in France. We were not lovers but really close friends –travelling together to Egypt, Mexico, Germany etc. It all came to a sudden end in Lisbon, Portugal on the friday after Thanksgiving in November 2015. She abruptly decided to leave me. And I do mean abruptly. To me it ended like a sudden death in the family, at that time. On reflection the severe action on her part was a blessing to me because it made it clear our friendship was over. I was first angry, then had a sense of relief. I can now remember the good times we had together without anger and sorrow. The lesson is that everything must end and we should not judge events by their ending but the totality of the experience.

But the biggest surprise of my personal life came a few months later. Anne Crawford and I were divorced in early 1985 and were strangers ever since. I did become a "friend" on facebook in 2015 but we hadn't spoken or seen each other for 30 years when a mutual friend told me in late 2015 that Anne suffered from Lyme

Disease. Somehow that touched my heart where my love for her had been lingering all those years. So I called her just to offer to help if I could. I did think of a small item and we started talking on the phone very gingerly.

The big surprise came in January of 2016. She volunteered to come to D.C. and take me to lunch on my 90th birthday! It was the best birthday gift any 90 year old guy ever got. Seeing her (and now every time we now speak) makes me feel really good-- t I didn't lose that lovely person after all.

Anne and I are friends. Having her back in my life, going places with her, and just talking on the phone makes me happy and appears to be O.K. with her.

So it's never over.

APPENDIX A
THE LIFE OF MORRIS FREEMAN, MY DAD

(Written by his son while sitting shivah right after he passed away)

Morris Freeman was born in Yakostov, a small village in the part of Russia that later became Lithuania, on the fifteenth day of Elul in 1885, which was August 26 that year. His father was the head of a yeshiva in that city, a Chasid who was a follower of the Lebovitzer Rebi. While not a rabbi, his father was a very learned man in the Torah who wanted his son to become a rabbi. His father was outspoken and criticized the community when he thought they were doing wrong, risking his own job. My father loved and admired his father, perhaps more than his mother, who, because of their extreme poverty, could not provide him with clothes and things he wanted.

My father began to study Jewish literature and the Torah very early in his home and in local Hebrew schools. He was a very good student. When he was in his early teens, the family moved to Anekst, a somewhat larger village in the same general area in Lithuania. He had only one brother, Chaim, who became a watchmaker. My dad continued his studies and even took over teaching when his father became ill and went to a mineral springs in Cameroon, near Riga. He was fourteen at the time. Many of my father's students were older than he was.

A year or two later, he went away to Slabotsky Yeshiva in Kovna. He had little or no money and, like the others, "ate-teg"—that is, got his meals by eating at a different home each day. Daddy was a student at Slabotsky for a year, and during this period, he became interested in Zionism and worldly issues. He once stayed up all night waiting to see a train on which Theodor Herzl rode through Kovna. Once for Purim, he sang "Hatikvah" at the yeshiva, and because of this and the literature he possessed about Zionism, the rabbi who believed that the state of Israel should await the coming of the Messiah dismissed him.

After leaving Slabotsky, Daddy became a young teacher in the city of Toukim near the large city of Riga, where he became acquainted with Jewish scholars. He was a close friend of Rabbi Kook, who later became the chief rabbi of Israel. Daddy walked in the woods with Rabbi Kook, and he enjoyed the beauty of nature in the winter woodlands. The rabbi asked Daddy to go to Israel with him, but Daddy, who was a worker Zionist, chose the United States instead. Daddy was more interested in his Socialist ideas and freedom, which he thought would exist in the United States. The idea of a Jewish state seemed too remote to him at the time. Later, in 1959, Daddy visited Rabbi Kook's yeshiva when he was in Israel, and though Rabbi Kook was long deceased, his daughter, who was eight years old when Daddy had left Europe, remembered Daddy, and he established a loan fund at Rabbi Kook's yeshiva to help the needy.

Daddy was about seventeen when he left the yeshiva and taught students. In Tookim, Daddy began teaching people on an individual basis, saving his money in order to go to America. He was already a Socialist and opposed to the Russian government, and his next three years or so were the period when his ideas for a better world were formed. He had no intention of serving in the army for the Russian czar. The incident that persuaded him it was time to leave for the United States was the Russian police started to arrest him as a revolutionary, but two women said to the police, "He's no revolutionary; he's a rabbi's son," and they let him go.

Daddy's father generally opposed his radical ideas, but once, Daddy overheard his father tell his mother, "Maybe our son is right." But still, Daddy's father was very sad when he decided to leave for the United States. Daddy was an attractive young man and had plenty of chances to marry into a rich dowry, but he was more interested in freedom and the United States, so he wanted to leave Russia.

Daddy's years in Europe were years of extreme poverty, and he often went hungry. His parents were nervous people, and despite having a warm relationship with his father, he did not have a happy home life. There was no electricity or anything else of modern life. Rather than baths in each home, there was a community bathhouse in which the women bathed on Thursday and the men on Friday. In the bathhouse were big rocks and a big wood-burning stove. Hot water was poured onto the rocks. The men used branches to whip each other to improve circulation. Daddy used to tell a story about a man who left the bath on a cold day and was stopped by a friend, who said to him, "For your health, how was the bath?" and he replied, "If I take the time to answer your question, it will not be good for my health."

Daddy would speak of the excitement he felt when the first railroad was built near Anikst and how the whole town came out to see the first train. He also described how he stayed up all night reading Jules Verne's *Twenty Thousand Leagues under the Sea*. He also read Zionist literature and became interested in issues of Socialist justice. He read Karl Marx in Yiddish and other literature.

Daddy left Europe in 1906, when he was twenty, on a ship from Hamburg, Germany. At twenty-one, he would have been required to serve in the Russian army. He traveled on the money he had saved from teaching. He needed fifty dollars to gain entry to the United States. Daddy's last name in Europe was Freyman, but when he applied for his first citizenship papers, the girl suggested a translation to Freeman, the English equivalent.

Daddy arrived in August 1906 and first lived in Worcester, Massachusetts, near a cousin named Mr. Paul. Daddy went to work in a skate factory for three or four dollars a week. His desire for personal freedom didn't fit into a mass-production assembly line. He walked off the job when someone called him a Jew and tried to discriminate against him. He got a job in a shoe factory next. He met many young people and pursued his Socialist ideas.

One evening at a party where he was the center of attraction, he met a man in the umbrella business who offered him a job as a peddler. The first morning, he sold all the umbrellas, about a dozen, by noon with a commission of ten cents each. He earned $1.20 in one morning.

After working for his original umbrella employer for some time, Daddy went out on his own, both selling and fixing umbrellas. He first went to the opera in Boston when a person gave him a ticket when he saw him standing in front of the Boston Opera House, selling umbrellas. Also in Boston, Daddy had a girl who loved him, but he wasn't interested in marriage. Daddy later recalled hearing Eugene Debs speak in Boston Common. He was a pale Zionist—a labor Zionist.

Daddy moved to Chattanooga, Tennessee, because his cousin Steinman wrote to him that it rained all the time there and they didn't have an umbrella man. So in 1913, he moved there. He rented a room with Mr. and Mrs. Nonin, who became lifelong friends, and lived there for six years. In Chattanooga, at first, his business was door-to-door peddling. He worked out of Mr. Nonin's store, a tailor shop. He continued working from this location for eleven years, until 1924, even though the tailor shop changed owners. He had no difficulty supporting himself through his umbrella business, although he told me that his Yankee accent caused some trouble in the post–Civil War South.

Daddy collected money for World War I refugees, which benefited his future wife, although he, of course, didn't know it. He was a pacifist and opposed to the war. Daddy said he was too young for World War I and too old for World War II. Actually, he was drafted during World War I, but the war ended before he left the induction station. While we are not certain, he probably never was actually legally inducted into the armed forces.

Daddy became the leader of the Workmen's Circle, a Jewish Socialist outfit, and traveled throughout the South to conventions and organized activities. The Workmen's Circle was the center of Daddy's life for his first decade in Chattanooga. Daddy helped workers in Chattanooga organize the moving-picture operators union. There were many lectures, meetings, and discussions in the Workmen's Circle, which absorbed most of Daddy's time and where he pursued his Socialist ideas.

The Workmen's Circle was an idealistic group that preached equality, peace, brotherhood, and labor rights. Promoting the Yiddish language was another major objective. Their meetings were in Yiddish. They sponsored Yiddish theater, in which Daddy was one of the actors, once playing the role of a *shadchan* (matchmaker). In 1924, Daddy helped start a major effort to form a Yiddish children's school after they failed to persuade the Hebrew school to add Yiddish to their agenda. Mr. Spector, a close family friend, was the leader of the Hebrew school who refused. However, the friendship survived the strain, mostly through the wives. Daddy also led an effort to establish a cemetery for the Workmen's Circle because the regular synagogue would not let the Workmen's Circle members get buried in their cemetery.

In the early 1920s, Daddy felt somewhat disillusioned with the Workmen's Circle. It was in this frame of mind that he first met his wife-to-be Lena Matzkel, on October 28, 1923, in Dalton, Georgia. The matchmaker was a Mr. Schwartz, whose family lived in Chattanooga near Daddy. Mother had to leave the next day for Atlanta to help her sister Helen give birth to Sylvia, which happened the next morning. The next day, Harold Noveck got diphtheria, and Mother was quarantined for the next two months.

Daddy and Mother met next in Atlanta in December 1923. They met several more times, and while Mother and her sister were visiting Daddy at the Workmen's Circle banquet and workshop to start the Yiddish school, at which Daddy spoke, unbeknownst to Mother and Daddy, her sister announced their engagement in the Chattanooga paper. The next day, Mother saw Daddy's store and was surprised that he only had a corner in someone else's store.

They also went to Lookout Mountain and took some pictures, which we still have.

Mother's family put considerable pressure on them to break off the engagement. She did so after paying him a visit in the spring, and then later in the year, she sent a letter asking to make up, a letter in which Mother forced Uncle Louis, my aunt Ella's husband.to write that he forced her to break up with Daddy. Daddy met her in Atlanta. They went to Grant Park, talked, and went to a symphony concert. The wedding then took place in Atlanta at Aunt Helen's home on March 15, 1925. (Aunt Helen had stopped a previous rendezvous when she locked the door and talked Mother out of going to the station to meet Daddy on a trip to Savannah.)

In the spring of 1924, a big fire occurred in the tailor shop where Dad was located and burned all the umbrellas. Daddy had to pay his customer's for their lost umbrellas, since he had no insurance. At that time, a Mr. Silverman, who had the agency for White Swan Laundry, asked Daddy to join him. Shortly thereafter, Mr. Silverman committed suicide, and Daddy took over the laundry. Later, he added a dry cleaning agency, a ladies' hose area, and a men's haberdashery, and he still sold and fixed umbrellas. He stayed in this same location at 5 East Ninth Street until 1954, when he retired from business.

Before he married, Daddy's reputation in Chattanooga's Jewish community was that of an idealist who was not capable of settling down and making money. The family pressure on Mother not to marry Daddy resulted from such stories. After his marriage, Daddy worked regular hours, 7:00 a.m. to 7:00 p.m., in the store, coming home for lunch. Gradually, he gave up his leadership role in the Workmen's Circle and finally pulled out altogether in 1928. His interests shifted to family life and business. Others in the Workmen's Circle felt that he had deserted their cause, but Daddy had years ago felt that most of them were not sincere.

In the period from Daddy's arrival in the United States to after his marriage, he did not practice Jewish religious observances. He was a radical who had little or nothing to do with organized religion. He was a free thinker. He was perfectly agreeable to Mother being religious, but he was not observant. Even in the early years of his marriage, he kept his store open on the Jewish High Holidays, although he stayed home and did not attend services. He escorted Mother to the synagogue the first year but did not enter, perhaps because his Socialist friends would say he had sold out.

In the years 1925–1929, Daddy's business gradually grew, and he made a nice living. David was born on January 14, 1926, ten months after the wedding. Daddy was extremely happy, a very proud father. He bought Mother a diamond ring—previously, she had only had a wedding band. There were several subsequent miscarriages until Harold was born seven years later.

Daddy's love for his children was strong and constant. David used to wait to have lunch until his daddy came home. They had no family car, but they took streetcar trips to Warner Park, East Lake Park, and Mission Ridge. When Sunday movies began, they became a regular family event.

The Depression began to hit in the early 1930s, and debts piled up. In 1931, the family moved to a cheaper apartment on Vine Street next to the railroad tracks. Daddy's main financial problem was a long-term lease on the store for his business, with rent at $125 a month. Daddy filed for bankruptcy in early 1933, primarily to reduce this rent, and his business continued.

On March 13, 1933, Daddy's second son, Harold, was born in the midst of the Depression. In May 1933, they moved to the country—Monte Vista Drive in Brainard, just off Germantown Road. They moved to save money and because the smoke from the trains was bad for David, who was suffering from asthma. They lived there for two years but had to move when the house they rented was sold. They moved to Rockaway Drive in Eastdale, also in the country.

The early 1930s were, of course, the Depression years, and it took a major effort to make a living. But Daddy did not forget about his ideals and his fellow men. He helped organize the Independent Lodge of Chattanooga, whose primary purpose was to loan money to needy people. The lodge had an annual supper and provided a death benefit to members. He helped raise money for the loan fund. He continued this activity until the lodge disbanded in 1950, when it was no longer needed.

Living in the country in the years 1933–1935 meant Daddy couldn't come home for lunch during the week. Bus service was hourly, at best. The family had no car. Mother sent him his main meal through Solomon Groceries, who delivered groceries daily to the house and then took Daddy's meal to him, often as late as 2:00 or 3:00 p.m. Then Sunday was Daddy's day of rest and enjoying his family. There was little contact with organized religion. The rural area was hard on Daddy and lonely for Mother but offered David fresh air, woods, a flowing creek nearby in which to play with the Watkins family kids, blackberry picking on a nearby hill, and stories about Indians.

Upon moving back to town in 1935, Daddy joined the B'nai Zion Synagogue, and David started Hebrew school. Daddy also joined the Arbiter Farband, a Zionist organization with a social welfare outlook. He became active in the organization but did not have a leadership role, and he became inactive after several years. He began attending religious services in the late 1930s after moving back to town.

Daddy's business gradually improved. Beginning in 1938, Daddy took off for two or three weeks and went alone to Hot Springs, Arkansas, for an annual vacation. David helped out in the store to facilitate such trips. David and Harold worked in Daddy's store on Saturdays and after school. When Mother and Daddy married, Daddy wanted Mother to stay home, but even in the first years, she worked during the Christmas holidays. When Harold was five, in 1938, she would come down to the store on a rainy day or when Daddy was on vacation.

David's bar mitzvah in January 1939 was a high point of Daddy's life. He closed the store that Saturday. Mother's father came from Atlanta, and both of her sisters, Helen and Ella, also came. There was a big reception in the synagogue after the ceremony. The rabbi, Daddy, and Mother's father gave speeches. All their friends were invited, and most came, except some businesspeople. David's Bible teacher from school, Mrs. Flynn, came. On Sunday, there was a party at Daddy's apartment. Mrs. Nonin was the biggest help in preparing for the bar mitzvah. Mother had a miscarriage only two months before that, and she was still weak.

Daddy had received word in 1930 that his father died. He had sent money to his mother and brother and continued to send about ten dollars a month to them. His brother was married and had a daughter who was about David's age. When his father died, he asked his mother to come to the United States, but she refused, wanting to be buried next to her husband. When World War II broke out, they thought about moving them, but Daddy didn't visualize the Hitler horror and didn't take quick-enough action. His mother, brother, and entire family perished in the Hitler bloodbath, although Daddy never found out the details other than that his family was murdered by Germans. The fact that they could have conceivably been brought over before that happened was on Daddy's conscience the rest of his life.

The war intensified Daddy's lifelong interest in Zionism. He moved closer to religion. He tried to call on the Jewish community through the synagogue to have a big protest against the persecution of the Jews in Europe, but he was met with indifference and comments that it would cause anti-Semitism. But, of course, he, too, did not foresee the Holocaust.

Daddy tried to spearhead the establishment of a Jewish community center. A speech he gave sparked a drive to create one, when the Jewish community had no building but was instead renting. The drive resulted in the purchase of a house on Fourth Street right after the war. Daddy was on the board of the center for a couple of years, but he dropped out because the center didn't follow his ideas about religious content.

The war years brought better business, but Daddy did not have a car until 1946. Many of Daddy's customers were black, and they probably patronized his store because he treated them as equals. The family lived near black people from 1926 to 1946. When living on Rockaway Drive in the country, we saw hatred when a white neighbor burned down the home of a black man across the street because he dared to build his house on the same street. Mother and Daddy moved to town because they couldn't stand such hatefulness. The white man sent threatening notes; he was probably anti-Semitic too.

A hallmark of Daddy's life was his love of America and his hatred of Russia under the czar and Communist rule. He was a fierce anti-communist. His social-welfare ideas never flirted with Communism. The pact between Hitler and Stalin confirmed his hatred of both of them, and he predicted their downfall based on his undaunted faith that America and justice would prevail.

When David was about to join the merchant marines, Daddy made a special trip to Atlanta, where David was at Georgia Tech, to try to talk him out of it. He thought the merchant marines were more dangerous than the infantry into which David was otherwise going to soon be drafted. David was not persuaded. As it happened, many of David's contemporaries became infantrymen and were in the Battle of the Bulge.

Later, when David was in a hospital in Boston in 1944 to get his appendix removed, Daddy left his business to see him and bring him home. It was his first trip to Boston since he had left thirty years earlier. He saw his cousin Paul there and continued to write to him when he returned home.

Daddy paid for all of David's college expenses at Georgia Tech starting in 1943 and then from 1945 to 1948, when David did not receive GI Bill aid since the merchant marines were not yet legally recognized as veterans. His sons' education was always his highest priority, and he made no attempt to mold their careers in any way. When David reached a low point at Tech and was on the verge of flunking out, Daddy stood by him and encouraged him to continue, and he did. He never complained about the financial support and even indulged his son by giving him a car his senior year, the first family car.

Harold's bar mitzvah in March 1946 was another happy event. However, the recent tragedy of his family was still fresh in Daddy's mind, and when he spoke, he wept freely. For the rest of his life,

Daddy stayed determined that the six million Jews killed by Hitler should never be forgotten.

In politics, the Democratic Party under Franklin Roosevelt became the champions of Daddy's social and humanitarian ideas, so he was a great admirer of Roosevelt's. Daddy probably voted for Norman Thomas, the Socialist candidate, in 1932, but after that, Daddy always said that it was Roosevelt who made Socialism live on. With Roosevelt, he became a Democrat, and he supported Democratic candidates for the rest of his life, except when he voted for Eisenhower in 1952, but not in 1956, because he thought there was corruption that a change in parties needed to clear out.

Daddy used the local press as a means of airing his views and advancing his ideas about patriotism and issues of the day. He started writing letters to the editor in the late 1930s, and there were interviews and feature stories about him from time to time. These continued the rest of his life. His letters stressed his love for his country, his pride, and his appreciation for his own success and his children's success. He also stressed the cause of Israel.

The tragedy in Europe hovered over the postwar years for Daddy, but he did not become morose. His business was still good in those years. He became more religious. Sunday was for rest, movies, and occasionally friends.

In the spring of 1948, Daddy closed the store one day so he and Mother could attend Harold's graduation from junior high school; a teacher had alerted them that Harold was receiving a medal. Later in 1948, David graduated from Georgia Tech in Atlanta, and Daddy and Mother were proud to attend. At a dinner party for that occasion, Daddy and Mother met Marianne, David's future wife. Mother went to Florida for her first vacation right after the graduation.

In 1949, Daddy bought his first home in Brainard, at 103 North Lovell Street, where he lived for the rest of his life. He and Mother loved their home, which had a nice yard and was convenient to Brainard Road and the bus service.

David kept the family car in Knoxville, where he worked for TVA, till March 1949, when Harold turned sixteen and could drive.

Daddy, then sixty-four, had no desire to learn to drive. Harold drove Daddy to work in the morning and would take Mother and Daddy places on the weekend. The car was theirs till Harold left home in 1955.

In January 1950, David married Marianne in Athens, Georgia. It was a very happy occasion. David and Marianne lived in Knoxville. There were family visits back and forth every two or three months, sometimes more frequently. In September 1950, Daddy suffered a massive coronary. His condition was quite critical for several days, and the family all gathered together. He pulled through and began to return to the store for a few hours at a time by Christmas.

Daddy's personal habits were conservative. As a bachelor, he played a lot of pool and poker but did not drink or smoke very much. There were always liquor and wine in the house, but Daddy never became intoxicated. He stopped smoking altogether after his marriage and also gave up pool and poker.

Daddy had a pay phone in his store to discourage customers from using it. He would call Mother by ringing twice and hanging up, and she would then call him to save a nickel (later a dime). Thus, we never answered the phone till the third ring. His spending habits were frugal, but he was always generous with his children, who always felt that he would give them anything they really wanted. Accumulating money was never an end in itself; education and making something better of oneself and the world were the themes of the home.

A series of happy family events happened in the 1950s, when family life was the focus of his life. Harold gave him great pleasure in 1950 when he led the ceremonial parade at Memorial Auditorium as president-elect of the high school student body and senior class. He graduated with honors and awards a year later, in May 1951. Daddy and Harold worked closely together in the store in the early 1950s and got along fairly well, with occasional arguments. Harold wasn't interested in continuing the business.

After his heart attack, Daddy seldom returned to work after lunch. Mother and Harold ran the store. Daddy also developed cataracts in the 1950s, which were removed in Atlanta without difficulty. Harold worked in the store his senior year of high school (1951) and while going to the University of Tennessee at Chattanooga (1952–1955). They closed the store at 6:00 p.m., rather than at 7:00 p.m. as in the past.

Daddy finally retired in 1954, when the widening of Ninth Street eliminated his store, which he was still renting. He probably wouldn't have retired except that the Ninth Street construction forced relocation. He was sixty-nine years old. He was then eligible for Social Security, businessmen having only recently been covered. He didn't retire completely; with Mother's encouragement, he set up one room at home for repairing umbrellas, and many of his customers came to his home. Also, he would go to town on the bus and pick up umbrellas for repair at department stores, Electric Power Board, and other places that collected them for him.

After his retirement, Daddy started going to the synagogue and was quite active. He kept up a steady stream of letters to the editor. And there was a series of happy family events—the birth of Daddy's first grandchild, Anita, on March 6, 1954; Harold's graduation from the University of Tennessee at Chattanooga in 1955; the birth of his first grandson, Stan, on October 15, 1956, and his briss (the ceremony was not religious enough for him); and David's graduation from law school in Knoxville in December 1956, the first in his class. Also, Roger was born on November 15, 1959, and Daddy was the godfather at the briss.

Daddy's heart and eyes were fine, so in his retirement, his days were leisurely but busy. He watched TV and listened to the news many times a day. He was intensely interested in Israel. Customers would come, and he would work several hours a day and many days a week. Each customer paid a social visit in which philosophy and his stories consumed much time.

In 1959, Daddy and Mother took a trip to Israel to fulfill a lifelong dream, a trip Mother had wanted to take for a longer time than Daddy. They left for Israel in April and returned in July, traveling on Israeli ships. The trip was a success in every way. Daddy was extremely excited and happy on the ship there and in Israel. He met many like-minded people on the ship. In Israel, they went to Tel Aviv and saw Hebrew and Yiddish theater. They spent a day in Rabbi Kook's yeshiva. They met Simon Noveck, a rabbi who was Mother's nephew, in Jerusalem at a B'nal B'rith convention. They heard Prime Minister Ben-Gurion speak on the need for Jewish day schools in the United States, a view Daddy stressed. The ceremony was impressive. They visited many sights around Jerusalem.

On the return trip, Daddy and Mother were honored by the ship's captain as the best passengers and ate at the captain's table. The Chattanooga papers had write-ups on their trip. Then, when Daddy and Mother returned to the United States, they found a telegram that said Marianne was pregnant, so another grandchild was on the way. Also, Daddy found out that he had diabetes upon his return from Israel, but he got it under control through diet and pills.

Upon their return, Daddy found that a neighborhood synagogue had been established within walking distance of his home. He was unhappy with the B'nai Zion Synagogue downtown because of its emphasis on money and lack of any real religious atmosphere. Daddy was then becoming very observant as an Orthodox Jew. He joined the new suburban synagogue, Beth Shalom, and became a charter member and mainstay of the group. Daddy went to services almost every day; he would get picked up, because in later years, he couldn't walk that far. The synagogue and religion were the center of Daddy's life in his last decade. He continued to write letters to the editor and to visit his family in Chattanooga, in Washington, and later in Cincinnati.

A major event was Harold's wedding to Barbara on June 11, 1961, on Long Island. It was a big, beautiful, kosher wedding. The evening before, Daddy took us all to a kosher nightclub in New York City for a gala rehearsal dinner. He was a proud and happy host. Also in 1961, David and his family moved to Washington, which ended the frequent trips back and forth but resulted in annual trips to Washington and visits from them. The next spring, there was another grandson, Douglas, and a really traditional briss, which pleased Daddy, in his present religious attitude.

The years after that followed the same pattern—trips to Washington and Cincinnati, and Brian's birth and briss in 1966 in Cincinnati. Daddy was very proud of his sons and took great pleasure in following David's rising career in Washington and Harold's in Cincinnati. He enjoyed visiting his sons' large homes and seeing his grandchildren—visits that were happy interruptions to a quiet but happy home life.

He took great pride in attending a Chattanooga luncheon in 1962 where David, who was then assistant to the Federal Power Commission chairman, was the featured speaker; a picture in the *Chattanooga Times* of Mother, Daddy, and David remains a prized possession. The *Chattanooga Times'* front-page coverage of a speech David gave in 1969 was another occasion of great pride, and Daddy's friends congratulated him on his son's achievements.

Daddy's last two trips were to Washington in 1969. In July, he went to the wedding of Cousin Raymond and his wife Zelda's daughter, Sandra—a real Chasidic wedding that Daddy thoroughly enjoyed. Perhaps the capstone of his life was Stan's bar mitzvah in November 1969. Daddy was still in good health, and he thoroughly enjoyed the occasion. There was a dinner afterward at the National Press Club with Jewish music by a cantor. Daddy spoke, and his speech, which stressed his love of his country and his sons and his joy over the occasion, brought tears to the eyes of the government officials and other guests and a standing ovation from them. He clearly captured the hearts of everyone there with his vitality and obvious pride in himself, his family, and his country.

Harold and his family and David made visits in Chattanooga in the ensuing months. David stopped over for two days in late May 1970, and his grandson Stan paid him a five-day visit in July. Stan went to the synagogue with Daddy and made the tenth man for a *quorum* (minion) one day. They walked and talked together, and Daddy lined up a playmate—Louis Epstein's son—for him at the synagogue.

Daddy's last illness began on the evening of Saturday, August 8, and he was hospitalized at Chattanooga Memorial on August 9, 1970. He became quite ill on the eleventh; two thousand cubic centimeters of fluid were drained from his lungs. Harold and his family rushed back from vacation, and David traveled nonstop from Europe upon learning the news on the thirteenth. Mother was with him constantly. The diagnosis was cancer, but Daddy was a fighter, and by Sunday, August 11, he was much improved, and during the next week, he steadily gained strength and was moved to St. Barnabas Nursing Home. Marianne, Anita, Stan, and Roger came over the weekend of August 23, and Daddy joked about how Stan would read a book with one hand and eat cookies with the other while visiting him in July. He said Stan was our best eater and sleeper.

There were many opportunities for conversation in those last days of August. He told David that he should "enjoy life; it was to be a joy" but that all people should "stand for something bigger than themselves; don't be wishy-washy." He maintained a keen interest in Israel, the status of the ceasefire, and world events. During those last weeks, he exhibited paranoia to a much greater extent than in the past, although he always strongly felt he was unloved and rejected by the world at large, not his family. He had illusions of threats to David, his wife, and his home.

Harold, and some of his family, stopped by for several days from August 23 to 26, just as David returned to Washington. Since there was hope that Daddy would live for months or longer and the family doctor, Dr. Livingston, said the trip was not a problem, Mother, David, and Harold decided to move Daddy to Cincinnati. Otherwise, Mother would live alone, traveling back and forth on the bus each day with all the problems of needing nurses and having no backup for emergencies. Also, the Jewish hospital where Daddy was moved to had kosher food and better nursing care.

An ambulance moved him on the Sunday of Labor Day weekend. He grew worse on September 8, but after the fluid was drained that evening, his condition gradually improved on the ninth and tenth and the morning of the eleventh. Harold was there in Cincinnati, and David arrived on the morning of the ninth and stayed for two days. Daddy's doctor, Dr. Silver, said he appeared to be improving and advised David to return on the afternoon of the tenth, and indeed, Daddy did continue to improve the next morning. David's afternoon good-bye was a sad one for him, for he knew that the diagnosis was correct and it was only a matter of time, although they had hopes that his time would not be so short.

That afternoon, Daddy joyfully acknowledged the news that Supreme Court nominees G. Harrold Carswell and Orval Faubus, two racists, had been rejected. He expressed the hope that someday there would be a Jewish president and vice president—not at the same time—and a black president and vice president. He continued to long for a peaceful world, and one where brotherly love prevailed.

The end came with a sudden heart attack at noon on September 11, 1970, which he never knew hit him. The doctor had left him only an hour or so previously. Mother was with him at the time.

The funeral was on Sunday, September 13, and he was buried in Cincinnati, where Mother moved to be with family. This unlikely resting place recalls one of Daddy's favorite stories, which he often told: "A great rabbi was walking down the street one morning when the king passed by and said, 'Good morning, Rabbi. Where are you going?' The rabbi replied, 'I don't know.' The king said, 'What do you mean?' and when the rabbi persisted in his answer, the king felt insulted, saying surely the rabbi knew where he was going, and thus, the king put the rabbi in jail. The king visited the rabbi in jail and said, 'Why did you refuse to answer me?' to which the rabbi replied, 'I really didn't know. I was walking to the synagogue, but you see, I landed in jail, so one really doesn't know where he is going.'"

The funeral ovation was given by Rabbi Simon Noveck, Daddy's beloved nephew who helped hold the chuppah at Daddy's wedding in Simon's home in Atlanta and was a lifelong spiritual comrade; Simon was a liberal too. Rabbi Needle, who had been Daddy's rabbi in Chattanooga for the past four years, had, by chance, just moved to Cincinnati, so he officiated and also spoke.

All of Daddy's immediate family—his wife, sons, daughters-in-law, Anita, Stan, and Roger—attended. Mother's sister Helen; Harold's wife, Sydney; and Sylvia came down from Detroit. Mother, Harold, and David sat shivah through Friday, September 18, 1970, the period when this story was written by his loving son.

APPENDIX B
MY MOM

(Written by his son while sitting shivah after she passed away)

Mom passed on February 2, 1988, at age ninety, after suffering two severe strokes on December 24, 1987. Harold and I are sitting shivah—a period of mourning and remembering Mother's epic life, much of which is contained in my story of Dad's life. I will try to recall some of her pithy, witty expressions.

When she was ninety, I asked Mother, "How do you feel?"

She said, "I hope you find out someday."

On Mother's Day a couple of years ago, Mother and I were speaking on the phone. After a while, Mother said we were talking too long; it cost too much. I said I could afford it. She then said, "If you have money to waste, please hang up and give it to Israel."

At age eighty-five, she had a nosebleed. I asked her later if she worried about it happening again. Mother said, "Oh, I hope so. You know they happen every five years."

A couple of years ago, I asked Mother what she thought of President Reagan. She said, "Some good, some bad."

"What has he done good?" I asked.

She said, "President Reagan has been good to Israel."

"And what has he done bad, in your opinion?" I asked.

"He cheated you out of three thousand dollars."

"Oh, Mother!" I said, with the disgust of a son who thinks his mother is really wrong. "What are you talking about? That's crazy!"

Unimpressed, Mother said, "It's sad, my son, that at your age, you can't remember what you told your own mother."

"What are you talking about?" I said with feeling, walking further out on a limb.

She then gently said, "You were TVA chairman when Reagan became president. He named someone else, and your salary went down three thousand dollars as just a director. You told me." I had completely forgotten, but not my mother, whose book on Reagan reflected her interests: Israel and her family. We had a huge laugh at my expense.

At the senior citizens' home one day, during Mother's last year, a busybody named Mrs. Gordon shocked Mother by telling her that her grandchildren had three different fathers, instead of just my brother Harold. Mother had never heard such talk in her life but didn't answer on the spot.

The next day, without asking anyone, she walked up to Mrs. Gordon and said, "Mrs. Gordon, you know what you told me yesterday? Well, my son Harold will be here Sunday. You tell him. He should know." Mrs. Gordon never bothered Mother again.

A couple of weeks later, Mother was in a car with my brother Harold's wife, Barbara, and in a very still voice, she whispered, "Can a man David's age still have a sex life? He's not married. What does he do?"

Barbara said, "Why don't you ask Mrs. Gordon?" And Mother had a great laugh, still concerned about her son's sex life while she was ninety.

Mother was quite pragmatic about death and had absolutely no fear. Dying was part of living for her. She once said, "It really wouldn't work out if we all just kept living. There wouldn't be enough food for everyone." She said she moved into the Jewish old-age home because Harold was nervous about her. She said, "He doesn't realize it's not like a cold; you only die once." Mother also said, "Living and dying go together. By ninety, you have already done most of your dying. There isn't much left."

Mother hardly ever spoke about such things as sex and only did so indirectly and in a whisper. When she lived in a Cincinnati apartment in her seventies, she had an upstairs bachelor neighbor who had women guests, and Mother could hear the bed rattling. She once whispered to Barbara, "I know what's going on up there. They aren't fooling me." But that's all she said.

Mother was most persistent and true to her religious practices even when this conflicted with her love of spending time with her children and grandchildren. One Chanukah, Barbara was not handling the candle lighting the way Mother felt was right. Barbara finally said, "Well, this is the way it is going to be done in my home."

Mother then said, "Honey, if there were bus service here, I'd take the bus home right now." Mother mellowed somewhat over the years and tolerated our way of doing things, but she held fast to her own observances to the very end.

Mother never lied, but she didn't believe in being a fool either. Mother's great fear was that her sons might get killed in a war, so you can imagine her reaction when a notice from the draft board arrived in the mail for her son Harold when he was in Cincinnati. Mother immediately threw it away and said nothing to Harold. Years later, Harold found out that it was a notice he was reclassified to inactive status, since he'd already been in the army. But Mother wasn't about to send a message to the military.

Mother was not impressed with new technology. She thought the space program was a complete waste of money. When the *Challenger* spaceship exploded, she said, "What was the purpose? Were they trying to improve the heavens?"

For Mother's ninetieth birthday, I thought long and hard about a gift since Mother did not want money wasted on material goods. I bought her a modern telephone, one that had preset numbers so that with one punch, she could call Harold or me. I thought it would make life easier for her. After I brought it to her room and explained it, she said, "Son, you're not the telephone man. Please leave my telephone alone. It's important to me."

I then explained to Mother that AT&T was broken up; people owned their own phones, and she only needed to push one number to call Harold. I plugged in the new phone. I said, "Look, I'll just push one number, and we'll reach Harold."

Mother was not impressed. She said, "That telephone doesn't know who I want to call."

I said, "Watch, I'll show you," and pushed Harold's preset number. As luck would have it, no one was home. Mother simply shrugged with a knowing look. That was the end of the new phone.

Mother could be persuasive—sometimes overly persuasive. While I was TVA chairman, Mother was interviewed by a reporter and photographed for the TVA newspaper. A really beautiful interview and article resulted. The reporter told me the photographer had a beard and, while serving them gefilte fish, Mother asked the photographer, "Are you Jewish?"

The fellow didn't have the nerve to say no, so he said, "I could be," and ate the fish.

Mother really didn't accept modern relations between men and women. She once said to me, "Son, you're a fool to keep paying Marianne alimony. Don't you know she has remarried?"

I said, "Mother, where on earth did you get that idea?"

She said, "From your daughter, Anita, who told me Marianne went on a trip to Europe with a man. And I know Marianne is a good woman, and she would never go on a trip with another man if she wasn't married to him." I laughed, and Mother just gave in.

About a year later, she learned that Marianne and this man bought a house together. She then said, "Now, what more proof do you need? A blind man should be able to see it now." I didn't try to explain that they still weren't married. Mother did comment once that modern women get more divorces because they have so many choices. In the old days, women could not even consider divorce; they couldn't support themselves. She was happy to be an old-fashioned woman in that sense.

Mother hated waste of any kind. She always turned off the lights and those kinds of things. During the last year she lived in the old-age home, she would take all the bread left in a wrapper once it was thrown away, tear it to bits, and feed it to the birds outdoors. She loved watching the birds, and they, too, shall miss her.

Mother could make her point of view rather sharply at times. Once, about five years ago, I was giving a speech in Cincinnati to the Sierra Club. Mother came with me. She sat in the front seat of the car of the young outdoorsman who took us to the speech's location. He asked Mother where she lived before Cincinnati, and she said Chattanooga. He then asked her, "How are you adjusting to our harsh winters?"

She said, "Quite easily, since I grew up in Siberia." The poor kid didn't say another word.

Mother taught me gratitude and acceptance of life's ups and downs. Most of all, she taught me to laugh. It was not until my dad passed away that I began to realize what a strong, wise, and independent woman my mom was. During World War I, the Russian government evicted her and her father from their home in a Lithuanian village just because they were Jews. They were taken by rail all the way to Siberia. They survived the bitter cold and, like refugees, wandered back home after the war. Mother then, in 1923, came to America with her father to join two sisters in Atlanta.

Mother had no use for American sports. She would often tell me she couldn't understand why Harold went to football games all the time. She once said, "Morris"—my father—"was a good, patriotic American without going to the football games." She expressed her distaste for the attention given to football in interesting ways. For example, over and over again, she would describe with pleasure how Anita once, as a little girl, saw a football game on TV and said, "Look at all those dogs running around!"

Mother made no attempt to understand or even use modern gadgets. They were all wastes of money to her. The TV's remote control was beyond her comprehension, so she didn't use it. Shortly after Barbara and Harold were married, when Mother still lived in Chattanooga, Harold got her a Sabbath light that a timer turned on and off so she could have a light on the Sabbath without violating her faith, which forbade turning a light on or off. After fifteen minutes of explanation, Harold became somewhat frustrated, so Barbara took over, with an air of certainty. After another fifteen minutes, she, too, failed. Mother just wasn't interested in doing something she didn't comprehend. Mother also never really comprehended the intercom in her apartment. She didn't realize you could talk back, but she did learn to let people in—all that was really needed.

When Mother and Harold went grocery shopping on Sunday—something Harold did religiously for a great many years—Harold would often stop first at a "money machine," an ATM, to get cash. When he told Mother what he was doing, she would say, "Son, you can't fool me. That machine isn't going to give you any money." Mother also laughed when we told her the car was saying to buckle up when it beeped.

Mother loved her grandchildren and great-grandchildren. Being with them in Cincinnati was the great joy of her later years. Mother learned enough about her grandchildren's interests to have conversations with them. But all she knew about Harold's son Mitchell's interests was he liked sports. The distinctions among football, basketball, and baseball were more than Mother cared to learn, so she would simply ask Mitchell about playing *ball*. Harold's other son Brian's interest in Israel pleased her.

Mother loved to tell this story of Harold's gentleness. When Mother first moved to Cincinnati, she lived with Harold and Barbara for two months. Then she moved into her own apartment. Brian, who was then quite young, went over to her before they left her alone the first night and said, "Please don't take a bath or shower by yourself. You might fall and hurt yourself." Mother was not afraid, of course, but was quite touched by his thoughtfulness. She lived alone in her apartment till she was eighty-nine.

Brian recalled that when he took Mother shopping instead of his dad in later years, she insisted on finding the items on her list herself, but she assigned him one or two items. She shopped in the order she wrote the items down on her list and never bothered to remember where they were located in the grocery store.

Mother was a lifelong supporter for black people. She often quite seriously told me that she had no problem with any of us marrying a black woman as long as she was Jewish. Once, sitting by the swimming pool at her apartment complex, she overheard two women complaining to each other because a black lady was in the pool. After the black lady left, Mother walked over to the two women and said, "Look, the water didn't turn black. It's clean." Mother used to sit down next to black people on the bus in Chattanooga, long before Rosa Parks and civil rights issues came to a head.

Mother was truly a humble person. She overestimated the opinions of others and greatly underestimated her own abilities. But she stuck to her beliefs—her religious roots—and was unshakable in her adherence to religion. She felt David made a bad mistake when he married Anne Crawford in 1984, and she refused to go to the wedding or to give her blessing in any way. She was, of course, very polite to Anne when she visited. When the marriage dissolved after a short time, Mother was quite candid in telling me she was glad. She did not pull any punches with me, but Mother could never say anything to her grandchildren that would hurt them.

When Anita and Hoppy decided to marry eight years ago, we worried about telling Mother. Anita and I went to Cincinnati to tell her together. Before we got to our message, Mother started talking about how her father objected to my father because he was not religious enough. Mother said, "I told him it could be worse—he could have been a Christian." She let us know later she knew what was coming. With Stan and Roger, her concerns were great when they married non-Jewish girls, but she certainly did not make either of them feel bad, and she enjoyed their visits.

She held out hope that their wives would convert so the children could be Jewish.

Mother was very charitable, but not if she didn't like the cause. She absolutely refused to join the old-age home's social club with dues of twenty-five cents a month because, she said, "They don't give anything to Israel." No amount of explanation that it was just for birthday parties. for the old people would shake her conviction that every Jewish organization should give to Israel.

She could be very clever in getting her point across. The community center—where she went most days—needed money for a new elevator. Mother saw no need for it since she never went above the first floor. She gave them ten dollars and told me, "They think I'm old and don't know that ten dollars is not much money, but the truth is that they don't need the elevator, and I don't want to give them very much."

Mother could be very stubborn. She rented an apartment, and the landlord offered to paint tenants' places and carpet their floors for one hundred dollars each. Every tenant but Mother took advantage of this obvious bargain. Mother claimed the walls were clean, even though she couldn't see well. She just did not want to spend the money.

Mother's humility and modest expectations are illustrated by my last visit with her at the old-age home in November 1989. We had a wonderful Sabbath together. She was happy talking about old times. I told her I'd be by early Sunday morning before going back to Texas. I came by on Sunday later than I said, and she said it was like getting a second visit. She assumed I had gone back to Texas without saying good-bye, but she wasn't angry about it. So we had another few hours together. Harold also came by, and we teased him about knowing Yiddish but not speaking it. And I did say good-bye.

She was a person who lived for her family and lived in her beliefs with humility and strength. As she once put it, "I'm going to blow away like the wind."

Printed in the United States
By Bookmasters